Oh HELL

A diary of war, dementia, love, and a glass or two of red wine.

By Pat Grayson

Published in 2017 by Heartspace Publications
Melbourne, Australia,
PO Box 1085 Daylesford, Victoria, 3460 Australia
Tel +61 450260348

www.heartspacebooks.com

pat@heartspacebooks.com

Copyright © 2017 Pat Grayson

All rights reserved under international copyright conventions. No part of this book may be reproduced, stored in a retrieval system, or transmitted in any form or by any means electronic, mechanical, photocopying, recorded or otherwise without written permission from Heartspace Publications.

Whilst every care has been taken to check the accuracy of the information in this book, the publisher cannot be held responsible for any errors, omissions or originality.

ISBN 978-0-9924338-4-0

V – Health & Personal Development

Dedication

This book is dedicated to the children and the children's children.

The print in this book has been enlarged for our older readers.

About Pat Grayson

Pat floats about. At the moment he is in southern Australia running a volunteer programme teaching storytelling and literacy to the indigenous community. He travels a lot, writes a lot, and helps new authors achieve their dreams of becoming a published author (www.writersangel.com).

Pat has written the following books:

> *Yogi, the tails and teaching of an alpha suburban doggy.*
> *How to write – right!*
> *Know ThySelf*
> *Oh Hell, of war, dementia, love, and a glass or two of red wine.*
> *Calling your happiness, a transformation story*
> *What would you do if you knew you could not fail?*

Should you want to contact Pat pat@heartspacebooks.com

Introduction

I started to write this book as a doodle, why not, as that is how I started writing in the first place. Yes a doodle but a cathartic doodle, one that was not meant to go anywhere except to the unfinished manuscript folder on my PC. But like a truck with a heavy load on a downward slope, it took off, faster and faster, not easily stopped. Of course it helped that periods of my family's history is interesting, but it was more than that.

There was a compulsion, an imperative that was larger than me. The story that needed to be told is one of insidious illnesses that affects a large percentage of the population of western society – the illnesses are dementia, depression, anxiety and panic attacks.

This is a story of people, real people, and how their lives were destroyed by these diseases. It is about the ravages of World War Two and Post Traumatic Stress Syndrome, and although my life has not been unduly affected by their diseases it is often a destroyer of the loved ones of the diseased.

As this is a story about people with various afflictions, I wanted it to remain about those people and so have not deviated with long medical descriptions or treatments, and have kept complex terminology to a minimum. And although I want to highlight the plight of those with the afflictions so readers can understand how sad and debilitating they are, it is a story and not a textbook, and so that is why I have kept complexity from it. The same with geographical detail and history, where I have given just enough to round out the story and not to flummox.

It is the real story of war, love, hate and disease – but more importantly, it is the story of life.

The mind is its own place, and in itself can make a Heaven of Hell, a Hell of Heaven ~ John Milton

Contents

Dedication	3
Introduction	5
In Gratitude	11
About 10th of June	12
Helen's Health and Mental State	13
11*th* June	19
12*th* of June	19
17*th* June	20
18*th* June	21
Helen's story	21
19*th* June	25
20*th* June	29
22*nd* June	31
Dad's story	31
Belgium and The Netherlands	35
France	35
June 21 – Smiley	37
More on Dad's history 39	
22*nd* June	43
23*rd* June	46
24*th* June	47
28*th* June	47
9*th* July	48
10*th* July	50
11*th* July	53
12*th* July	54
13*th* July	56
14*th* July	56
15*th* July	58

Me   59
    16th July   61
    18th July   63
    24th of July   66
    25th of July   68
    26th of July   69
    27th July   74
    28th July   77
    29th of July   78
    31st July   84
    1st August   85
    2nd August   87
    3rd August   89
    4th August   92
    5th August   97
    6th August   98
    7th August   99

My Story   103

In enters Enid   108
    8th August   116
    9th August   118

Shayne   121
    10th August   122

Hildegarde's (Hilda) Story   123
    11th August   129

Meeting the sisters   132

Zenon's Story   140
    12th August   144
    14th August   145
    15th August   146
    16th August   148
    17th August   150
    18th August   153
    20th August   153
    21st August   154

Other Resident's ... 155
    22nd August ... 157
    23rd August ... 158

Zoe's story ... 159
    24th August ... 161
    27th August ... 162
    26th August ... 163
    29th August ... 165
    30th August ... 166
    2nd September ... 167
    8th October ... 172
    10th October ... 173
    13th October ... 176
    15th October ... 178
    17th October ... 180
    31st October ... 180
    6th November ... 183
    8th November - Reflections ... 184
    26th November ... 185
    27th November ... 186
    28th November ... 186
    29th November ... 187
    1st December ... 188
    2nd December ... 188
    5th December ... 189
    8th December ... 190
    11th December ... 190
    16th December ... 191
    18th December ... 191
    21st December ... 192
    27th December ... 194

Final say ... 195

The funeral ... 196

Permission from Helen ... 197

Dad's eulogy ... 197

In Gratitude

I may have put the words down but this book is a result of the help from the following people. In many ways it is probable that this book would never have been written if it was not for the research and dedication that Shayne van Rensburg (my ex-wife and friend) produced. She spent many hours poring over records.

For the final clarity in understanding what happened to my father I am most gratefully indebted to Marcel (you will learn of his place in this story). If it was not for you there would have been too many gaps for Dad's story to be accurate.

And the same applies to my sister Sue Selic for her supporting information about our mother Hildegard.

Patricia Grundkowski (Zenon's last wife) for her interest and support. Deborah. Thank you for the support.

And lastly the players, my dad and Helen as unwitting partners.

About 10th of June

It all started when my daughter Kimmy sent me a text message saying: "Grampa (my father) is back in hospital. I don't know how bad it is, I'm trying to find out. It was Helen (Dads wife) who phoned me and of course she's frantic. If I find out more I'll let you know, love Kim".

'Hell', I know what this means. For now though I'm going to do my best to resist as I have been there before. But in my heart of hearts I know that I must go back to Australia and do what must be done. I arrived in South Africa only three weeks earlier on a two-month visit to my family and also to house-sit my son's place whilst he and his family were on holiday in Europe.

I SMSed Kim back and said that "I'll phone Helen and see how she is." I knew Kim was not going to be happy, as she would have liked me to have said, "OK, I'm on my way to take control", but for now it will have to do.

The minute Helen picked up the phone I knew that I could not unduly delay my return but I needed to until Lance and his family returned in another four days' time. As I talk to her, I know of old, the quivering voice and could imagine her hands shaking, claw-like as she works through a panic attack. As a result of her illness she has virtually no body fat, I could see her face with the shrunken-skin stretched drum tight, accentuating the protruding, pointed cheekbones, with her hazel eyes – small coffee beans in their large sockets. I know the despairing stare and the pain that those eyes contain. I could hear the tears in her eyes and I shudder.

Her words were incongruous with this memory as she says, "It's okay, ...I can... cope". We both know that she can't. I promised to phone back the next day and monitor her.

Helen's Health and Mental State

It started about six years ago. I had not been long back in Australia after living in South Africa for many years. With my periodic telephone calls to Helen and my father, I could detect that things were not quite right with Helen and made up my mind to phone more often. At that stage I was in Canberra and they were living near Devonport on a fifteen acre hobby farm.

Thereafter I started to phone every four or five days and with each subsequent call I could tell that things were deteriorating, where it seemed that she was losing control.

Helen was the strong one in the marriage and for the last forty odd years she was the one who did all the organising and made the decisions. I could see that things were running off the rails and so said to her, "Would you like me to come down for a while and help out?"

"No thank you. It'll be all right and you have your own life to live", which of course I do. Two days later my phone rang and I could see on the screen that it was Helen. The voice, anguished and trembling, and almost incoherent said, "Please, please, please come... I cannot cope".

The next day I was in Devonport and on their farm. This poor lady who was always so competent and capable was reduced to a quivering wreck.

We cannot understand the minds and lives of others and so we cannot see why some are more susceptible to stress than others, nor was it my place to query why she descended into this hell. But she did and it was real for her.

Trying to piece it together, I think it started with the general stress of life that affected her digestive system, which had sort of shut down. As this happened, she became even more stressed and the normal management of life became difficult and could not be handled and so stress built upon stress.

I have been interested in my health for many years and have read widely on the subject. I remember once reading of a lumber worker in Canada who, whilst working at the electric saw, had a piece of timber jammed between the saw and the gap in the table where the saw dust drops. But with the force of the saw the timber was catapulted out and into the man's side.

I seem to remember that this happened around the 1930's. The man was rushed to hospital and the local surgeon pulled the piece of lumber out leaving a gaping hole in the man's side. Peering into this, the surgeon saw straight in to the man's stomach. Amazed, he watched for a moment and realised that this was a unique opportunity, where for the first time ever, observation of the digestive process of a human was possible.

Somehow he convinced the man to become a research object and to remain in his surgery for observation. I can only assume that the convincing was done by way of the passing over of great sums of money. Nevertheless, for about two years, the man's stomached was observed. The surgeon sat and watched and recorded the goings-on as often as his time would allow and over the period he built up a very interesting study. What was most apparent was that when the lumber man became stressed, for whatever reason, that his food would not digest. The surgeon tested this on numerous occasions by inducing stress and then feeding the man, so as to observe the result. And although I read this many years ago the lesson that stuck with me was that when one is stressed, food takes literally three times longer to digest. Therefore, the food petrifies within the gut, thereby helping to poison the entire system.

This research as done in Canada was the starting point for digestive stress research and, over the years, it is been proven to be the case that when people are stressed they do not digest efficiently.

With a digestive system that had pretty much shut down, Helen's health was failing badly, exacerbating the situation. She went to the local GP (I met him at a later stage, he reminded me of that British comedian Benny Hill, and probably about as effective as Benny Hill would have been). And so the rounds of specialists started until one bright spark of a surgeon said, "Your gallbladder must come out". Of course she challenged this and said, "Are you really sure?" "Of course my dear, trust me, I am a doctor."

Helen, clutched at this glimmer of hope, and so the operation came and went, as did her gallbladder. The surgeon told her it would take three months before her digestion would improve. Three months came and the digestive system was just as clogged. Now the surgeon said, "Sometimes it takes six months." Six months came and the canals were still jammed. Twelve months later they were worse. Of course, nobody challenged the surgeon, he had been paid, and the file was likely to have been closed as another successful operation.

This was the situation when I arrived on the farm. Helen was unable to function in almost any area. I made another appointment with the GP, fat lot of good that did as he did not have a clue about panic attacks. But over a period of time we managed to get to see a couple of specialists. However, Helen had her own timeframe and one night when we all went to bed she took an overdose of tablets. Fortunately, that night Dad did not sleep well and he found her on the floor – just conscious. He came and woke me up. Luckily the ambulance arrived quickly and whisked her off to Emergency.

After pumping her stomach she was okay and she was kept her in a normal hospital ward, on sedatives and under observation.

After four or five days she was feeling a bit better and itching to come home. But the Tasmanian medical services saw it differently, where all attempted suicide cases are to be referred to the psychiatric ward. In this case that would be in Bernie, a ninety minute drive from the farm. Helen rejected this offer and firmly announced that she was going to go home. This was on a Sunday morning, and the hospital was fairly quiet. I had taken Dad to visit her as they had revoked his driving license. I could see that she was agitated and wanting to come home. I did not think that she would do anything stupid but she did as you will learn. Thinking I would give the two of them time alone I went for a walk, saying I would return in half an hour. When I did it was to a scuffle at the entrance of the hospital.

What apparently happened was that, after I had gone, Helen said to Dad "I want to go home." Of course Dad was well entrenched in his own dementia at that time, and so he encouraged her. Together, they pulled off all the leads that attached her to the monitor, and headed out the door.

One of the nurses saw them just as they were leaving and went to delay them. At the same time she called loudly for security. Within a moment or two there was a real kerfuffle with the nurse, a doctor who had arrived and two security staff all struggling with Dad and Helen. Helen had her arms wrapped around Dad as if welded to him. The security guard and the nurse were trying to separate them so that they could restrain Helen.

As I came through the door I heard Dad's voice shouting, "I vill kill you, let us go". I might add that when this happen Dad was eighty-seven years old, and Helen was about thirty-eight kilograms. As I ran to try and create some sense of normality in this scene I could hear the doctors say that it is a legal responsibility for her to go to the psychiatric ward and that she has no choice in the matter. At the same time Dad was trying to punch the burly security guard in the stomach.

When I got there, I shouted, "Stop, stop this nonsense", which initiated a slight pause in the scuffling as both Dad and Helen looked at me pleadingly to get these people to go away and leave them alone to go home. And when I told Helen that I had no control over this... you have to go with them, I could see the betrayal in their eyes, and so the scuffling started afresh. But finally we were able to remove Helen's arms from Dad's body and I was able to start pushing Dad towards the exit. But as I looked back I saw them dragging a kicking and screaming Helen back into the depths of the facility. I knew they were to heavily sedate Helen and that the ambulance would be called for to transport her to the Burnie nut house.

Getting Dad to and into the car was most difficult as he wanted to go back and kill those people who are taking his wife away. But little by

OH HELL

little I managed to pacify him by saying that we would go through to Burnie and see Helen later that afternoon.

Into the psycho ward she went, where she languished for two months – filling her up with drugs and concoctions, all meant to pacify. Of course I stayed on the farm to look after Dad. Daily we drove the three hour drive to see the old girl.

At that time Dad had pretty much given up red wine. This was at Helen's insistence because, according to her, his face was going 'red'. Poor old bugger was distraught without his lady and could not understand what was happening. So I reintroduced the wine, feeling it would do him more good than harm at this difficult time – we would deal with the red face later. Besides, at eighty-seven, who cared? Needless to say, a massive smile emerged when he saw the wine cask that I bought for him. For a time I was forgiven. When Helen was finally released and came home she was still a mess. The drugs she was still on only partially and spasmodically controlled her.

It was hideous seeing her in those moments of despair. Hunched over, staring at the floor, seemingly not comprehending anything, whilst her hands continued twisting and strangling a handkerchief. It went on for hours with tears and snot dripping on the floor. "Why am I alive… I've got no reason to live…" On and on, the handkerchief oblivious to its real purpose of mopping the face was rung and twisted, back and forth by those clawed hands.

Dad, the red wine confiscated, not comprehending what was happening, would sit there glum and say nothing. Whilst she rocked back and forth bemoaning her fate. I felt helpless and totally inadequate.

Needing to understand the situation, I made it my business to learn what a panic attack was; a sudden overwhelming feeling of acute anxiety, often accompanied by heart palpitations and shortness of breath (hyperventilating). At first I thought she was having a heart attack.

Over the weeks she improved enough to get by, I stayed a little bit longer and then left them to their life.

The next three or four years were difficult with no real recovery, but yet they were together on their farm for what was to be the twilight of their lives. Helen was brave and soldiered on. Dad faded fast, as did his memory and mind. Helen, still astute, knew that their days on the farm were coming to an end as they could not manage it anymore. The farm was put on the market and finally sold. This in itself created much stress for Helen, because of the selling process, all the documentation and then of course the packing and the actual move. To coincide with the selling of the house they bought a two-bedroom unit in Devonport. When they got there, it took Helen eighteen months to unpack properly, but even now, nearly four years later there are still boxes everywhere. But they were relatively comfortable and happy, that was until Dad had a heart attack. Back I went to Tasmania to see how I could help. They gave Dad three months to live, and so John, my brother, came across to see him.

Dad is a strong old buzzard and recovered enough to be let out and go back home. They then said he probably has another six months. That was eighteen months ago. Somewhere along the line he had a stroke, perhaps this was in his sleep because nobody knew it had happened until later on.

This was the environment that I would be re-entering if I was to go back to Tasmania. It was Hell last time and it would be Hell again. As it turned out I was not wrong.

OH HELL
11th June

I phoned Helen to see if there is any change. The dread is not so much about my father as his course is set – it is about Helen and how is she to cope. So the call is really to gauge the depth of her melt down. I am hoping against reality that she will get through this okay, but I know what the inevitable will be.

The minute I hear her voice I know that the inevitable is closer now than it was yesterday. Oh hell, I think once again, and although I know I must go, I try to delay it.

I ask her if she has managed to speak to a doctor as yet, she says "No, or if I did I can't remember". She tells me that Dad is unconscious and she doesn't know what's going on and if he will die or not.

Helen always has had a need to be in control and not knowing what is going on or what to do or how to help make her worse. The anguish through the phone sends a small chill down my spine.

12th of June

"Hi Helen it's Pat. How are you going, and how's Dad?" As before, I sense the pressure that she is under as she tells me that they are running tests on Dad. I learned later that was when they realised that Dad had had that stroke. But she does not really know what is wrong and no one will talk to her. They probably had, but she has forgotten.

It is times like these when she is at her worst. Helen is a lovely lady of great intellect and curiosity but over the last ten years she has been afflicted with anxiety and very little short-term memory retention. Some of the medical people mutter dementia, others talk about Alzheimer's, but at this stage they are only guessing.

17th June

"Helen, I will be there on the Saturday, I fly out from Cape Town tomorrow afternoon."

The sound in her voice was worse, and as I listened I realised why. Hospitals try to empty the beds as soon as possible, which is understandable. But if the person is old and is unlikely to ever return home (I was soon to learn Dad would never return home) they wanted to pass him on to an aged care facility. They had confirmed that he was advanced in his dementia.

We preferred the idea of a care facility because they would be better able to cope with him than a hospital. It would also be closer to home, in fact only a few minutes up the road. So Dad was transported and deposited in the place but when he got there he made such a rumpus and was so loud that he only lasted about eight hours and the ambulance was summoned to come in get him and return him back to the hospital in Burnie.

Helen was completely distraught, which is understandable. I needed to get back as fast as possible to try and sort this mess out. Later I was to learn that he was aggressive and threatening. Rude my father is, obnoxious, and yes loud; but for the love of me I have great difficulty in understanding how this ninety-two year old man, who is on death's door step, can be considered a threat – but they thought he was and so dispatched him.

So Dad was now back at Burnie hospital, very confused and even more delirious than what he was before.

Although my ticket was from Cape Town to Launceston, the journey it represented was so much more.

OH HELL
18th June

I landed at Launceston (Lonny) airport and hired a car to drive the one and a quarter hours to Devonport.

When I arrived there was a lady at the door, who I do not recognise. She tells me her name is Nola, and that she has been waiting for me to arrive so she can leave and return to her home in Brisbane. Nola, I learnt is Helen's niece from Helen's sister Jan, who is in an aged care facility about twenty kilometres away. Jan, it would seem has not been good, so Nola came to visit, staying with Helen. But when Nola realised how bad Helen was she decided to stay until I came to take over.

I was to learn later that Nola's intervention was really a great support to Helen and was with Helen for about a week before I arrived.

But here is the thing, Helen never told me about Nola being there. I was grateful that Nola had stayed to help but there was no reason for me to rush back from South Africa, as another day or two would not have made that much difference, especially when Nola stayed another three days whilst I was there. It seemed that Helen forgot to tell me that Nola was there.

Helen's story

Helen's was born into a farming family and community. Tallish and slim, always with snow white hair, straight like the hay they would have fed the cattle. This is cut short and combed forward with a straight fringe, like a young boy. And still, she is probably happiest when clad in dungarees and out working the land.

It was the thrift and practicality of a poor farming community that became her script for life. Geeveston, south of Hobart, is a pretty place but in those days it would have been fairly remote. The water for the once a week bath was warmed up by the copper (a copper drum with a gas flame underneath). In their young years, all three siblings bathed together, but later they bathed one after the other, all in the same water.

The farm was only about fourteen acres but required much hard-working to make it feasible. As one would expect on a farm in those days, all pitched in. I am not sure in the case of Helen's siblings but, always good natured, Helen would have enjoyed the work and be happy to contribute to the family welfare.

The farm was an apple orchid with several thousand trees, and from March through to April it was all hands on deck where thousands of apples had to be handpicked, sorted and boxed.

It was a hand to mouth existence because the apples would have been harvested and sold every April. There was one payment a year and that was at the end of the harvest. With that one payment, all previous credit was paid off, and for the following month there may have been a little bit in the bank account. But that would have soon been consumed and so for the next ten months they lived on credit and thrift. By all accounts the meals were fairly staid. The evening meal was meat and two or three vegetables per night. There was not much variety and what was consumed was what was grown in the area. Clothes were threadbare and darned on a regular basis to keep circulating for as long as possible.

For Helen growing up, this would not have been a hardship, as that was the way of it. Always a well read and curious person she gained great general knowledge. This coupled with her farming practicality endowed her many abilities from which to call on. And even now, with her condition as it is, that great knowledge and practicality is still evident.

At the age of twelve she went to board at a Christian school for girls. This was for five years. Although she thrived on the learning, she was not comfortable with so many other children. Many were from middle class families from Hobart, and she simply had nothing in common with them. After all, what would they know about blight or drought?

OH HELL

Life can be cruel in the way that it selects individuals to partake in events that are dished out specifically to them. When about twelve, Helen's mother started displaying symptoms that were most bizarre. Those symptoms were very similar to her own current symptoms. They are also similar to those that Dad has with memory loss and reduced cognitive function. Later, her mother was diagnosed with Huntington's disease, which in some way is similar to dementia, where brain cells trash, finally resulting in dementia. And so for Helen, as she witnesses the deterioration of her husband, where he becomes more and more mentally deficient, it is a rerun of what she went through with her own mother. Every time she goes to see Dad in hospital, it reminds her of her mother. The cruelty is; that probably the two most important people in her life have been reduced in the same way. This is often too much for her to bear.

It was not the Huntington's disease that finally ended her mother's life, it was cancer of the cervix. But Helen experienced the decline of her mother's health and mental function for about seven years until her mother finally died. One wonders if the cancer was a blessing in disguise as it ended that slow decline. But the downside would have been the pain and discomfort of cancer of the cervix. Either way it would have been hard on Helen's mother and of course it left an indelible mark on Helen.

Seeing her mother's decline as she did, would have been hard enough, but she lived in a time and community where things like ill-health were not openly discussed, and certainly not discussed with children – so Helen was not able to glean any compassion or support within the family, as all kept silent.

With her basic education behind her, she went to secretarial school. With this vocation, she found herself far away from the hard but interesting life of the farm and in an office. She was about as far out of the water as any fish could be. Whether it was part of her basic character or because she grew up on a farm, she was a bit of a loner, and so being in the office with dozens of chirping women (her description, not mine) was anathema to her. It is not that she does not like people, as she does enjoy positive interaction – she has the ability to respond to all levels of society with a generous nature. But, in her own words, "I just prefer my own company".

It was her curious mind that suggested she travel as much of the world as she could, and she did with many interesting tales and observations. So the intelligent girl of the farm became an intelligent girl of the world. But upon returning she had had enough of being in an office and chirping females, and so studied to become a primary school teacher. Once qualified, as per her need, it was the small farming and mining community of Savage River that she descended upon.

It was at Savage River she met Dad, each recognising the strength and the needs of the other. They would also have agreed that they had no need for society at large and would be happy in a small community, but separate from the community.

Their happiest time together was when they bought their fifteen acre hobby farm down near Port Sorell. It was on this farm that they worked at their separate chores, tinkering around for hours, but convening at tea breaks and meals to confer and share. With love and attention, the bland property became a home, and an orchard, with a place to sit and watch over the dam that they had created. Birds also found this little slice of paradise to their liking, with its indigenous trees and plants, to swoop and dive over the water in the never ending hunt for insects. When full, the birds took to the trees and chirped loudly to each other, much like at a Chinese garden market.

This farm, on this veranda is what they called home – it was here that they could just be.

OH HELL
19th June

Time to go and see Dad, so we jumped in the car at about 10:00am and headed to Burnie hospital.

I let Helen drive as I want her to retain as much capacity and for as long as possible. But I drove home, as she was shattered after to trip there and time with Dad.

My mind was on Dad as we scooted along the highway – will he have deteriorated much since the two months when I saw him last? As I was pondering this, Helen's words interrupted my thoughts... "About twenty years ago there was a fire along this section that totally devastated the bush. It was so bad that there was only dirt left ... houses were lost ... it was terrible. But it amazes me that it has recovered as it has. Nature is truly wonderful".

"Did it", I said. "Yes, it is amazing".

Since that time two months ago, Dad's deterioration was massive.

The first time I became aware of Dad's dementia was about two years ago when I came to visit. I came across on the boat, which gets in early and so I was at their place by about 7:30 in the morning. Although they knew I was coming, and the time of my arrival, they forgot and were asleep. I knocked on the door, and knocked, and knocked some more, and neither Dad, nor Helen heard. It was the middle of winter and there was frost and so I needed to keep warm and went for a brisk walk. I returned about nine and started knocking again, still nothing. But then finally, Dad who had woken, opened his curtains to let the day in. I position myself outside the window so he could see me, which he did. However, it did not sink in that there was a person there let alone his son. So I went back to the front door, where my knocking grew into banging. Eventually the door opened and there was Dad completely nude, on shrunken bowed legs. For some time he stared at me. I mumbled something like, "Thank God you've opened the door", but he kept staring at me in a curious way as he blocked the doorway. After a time he finally asked, "Who are you?"

The term dementia has a Latin derivative and basically means 'gone mad'. But of course the term was coined many centuries ago. Now, with the understanding that it is a disease it is wrong to call those people mad. However, it may be maddening to see the behaviour of your love ones with dementia.

The following description of dementia is from a book by Alzheimer's Australia: Alzheimer's disease is the most common type of dementia and causes a number of nerve cells in the brain to gradually reduce and the brain shrinks (this is a result of protein settling in the brain to become plaque). The nerve signals that are essential for activities, such as language and physical movement become increasingly impaired. The nerve cells can't be replaced so the functioning of the person living with Alzheimer's disease declines as more cells are destroyed.

In Dad's case he never made a conscious decision to relinquish aspects of life that make life worthwhile. For instance, there was never a decision that he would cease reading. He just slowly read less and less until he did not read at all. He stopped showing all interest in current affairs or watching the news, which was something that he had done all his life, not that he ever discussed current affairs. It was the same with going on short excursions with Helen, something that he enjoyed. A couple of years ago he just did not want to leave home. And because of his mobility issues, Helen bought him a seated scooter for him to whizz around in but he chose not to use it, preferring to sit in his lounge chair, immersed in his ever-growing nothingness.

Alzheimer's disease usually starts with forgetfulness, problems working things out, and difficulty in finding the right words (I might add opening the door to strangers with no clothes on). Family or friends may also notice changes in mood, where some may appear to be depressed.

As the disease progresses, memory loss becomes worse, and people have difficulty learning new skills and information. Changes may become more obvious with the progression of the condition where people say or do things that are out of character. Everyday tasks, such as getting dressed, washing, cooking, travelling and handling money may become difficult. Disorientation is also common and this can cause people with the disease to lose their sense of time and place, they may get dressed in the middle of the night thinking that it is morning. In fact, this was how Helen started to realise that something was wrong, when Dad often woke her up around one in the morning to ask if breakfast was ready. New surroundings and new people may be confusing and it could become difficult for people to recognise previous well-known family and friends. It was this, not recognising his new surroundings, was why Dad reacted badly when he was moved to the aged care facility.

During the late stages of the disease where impairments and changes are more severe, people with Alzheimer's disease may become totally dependent on others for their care.

James A. Michener in his book *Recessional* made the following statement; "As her mind disappears her body remains relatively strong, and we realize that she could be here for years, mind fading constantly, body failing more slowly but death refusing to knock on her door".

They had him seated in a wheelchair with a blanket on his lap. Incoherent mumbling emerged from a blank stare, as if he was reciting the contents of a tape recording that had been cut into a thousand pieces and ad hock selections had been used with no mind as to sequence. His head slumped slightly to one side and downwards, and so to see us as we walked in the door, his eyes look up in their sockets. There was a slight dribble on his chin and his hands shook constantly.

As we walked in he looked at Helen and there was recognition but he said no words to her – just the mumbling. Every so often he surreptitiously looked at me, and after a time I realised he curious as to who I was.

How unfair life is that people deteriorate like this at the end of their life. Would it not be better to crown a life if we went out proud and strong, instead of like this?

I went to try and find the doctor to get some sort of diagnosis on his condition and so went to the nurse's station and introduced myself. They said that he was on a calming agent as he was very disturbed, lashing out at all the staff. When I asked her if I would be able to see the doctor, she said that he had already done his rounds and that it was unlikely that he would return again today. It will be best if I come tomorrow at about 9 o'clock because that is when he is normally here. I thanked her and went into the coffee lounge to give Helen a bit of time with The Old Man on her own. I had my computer and so caught up with client emails.

On the way home, we got to that section of the highway, and Helen said, "About twenty years ago there was a fire along this section that totally devastated the bush. It was so bad that there was only dirt left. Houses were lost. It was terrible. But it amazes me that it has recovered as it has. Nature..."

"Wow, how amazing", I said.

That night was not a good night for Helen, which gave me an indication as to what was to come. She was unable to cook dinner and asked if I would. I was happy enough to do this, it gave me an opportunity to relax as I like cooking.

Helen collapsed on the settee and there was no movement from her until I called her to the table. She was unusually quiet and I could see that she was battling. I knew that the main part of my function here was to support Helen as best as I could and so I gently asked her how she was feeling. Upon hearing my words she literally dropped her knife and fork, her head bowed and started sobbing.

Girls are so much better at doing this than boys, and I was not sure what to do. There are arguments that suggest that you shut up and let the person speak. Or the other point of view is to talk gently to them to try and settle them. I covered the back of her hand with mine and said how difficult this was. Almost incoherently, she sobbed, "I hate seeing him like this... We must make sure that they do not keep him alive with unnatural means... Where is my husband, he's not there in that shell of a tattered body... Please, let him go quickly..."

20th June

After yesterday and last night Helen was not strong enough to make the drive through to Burnie. This made it easier because I needed to get there by 9 o'clock, and it would be difficult organising Helen to leave at 8 o'clock. She normally sleeps about eleven hours a night but this is probably due to the sedatives that she takes.

I was able to see the doctor, that is, the doctor of the day, because every time I saw one, it was a different doctor. He explained about the medication that Dad was on, and hoped that he would settle down over a few days. He said that he was not eating very well and went on to explain that Dad is in an advanced stage of dementia, and that he was slipping fast. He then asked me when did he have the stroke? When I shrugged my shoulders and said, "We weren't aware of him having a stroke". He replied, "Well there was one within the last week or so, perhaps it was whilst he was sleeping and no one was aware of it".

As mentioned before, two years ago he had a heart attack and was only expected to live a few weeks. Slowly he recovered to the point where he could return home and for that period of time, up until these last couple of weeks both he and Helen have had a moderately comfortable time of it. When I say moderately, I am not sure if that is the right term because clearly under Helen's facade the fear was building.

When I got home, Helen said. "We needed milk so I'll go shopping. I think that I'll also get a cooked chicken for dinner tonight". When she returned I helped her unpack and there was the chicken. But as I unpacked another bag, there was a second chicken. It would seem that she had bought the chicken and put it in the trolley and a few minutes later thought it would be a good idea to buy a cooked chicken for dinner, and so she did, again.

When I got to the end of the shopping bags I noticed there was no milk.

As the digits on the phone are difficult for Helen to see, I went and bought another one that had digits the size of dinner plates. I installed it and got it working. We just used it like an old-fashioned phone for a few days so she could get used to it. There was no problem. I then asked her if would she like me to put in the eight or so phone numbers she uses on a regular basis, such as her sister Jan's, into the phonebook? She said, "Okay, please". So I did and then went to train her on how to use the 'phonebook' and even wrote out the instructions. These were, press the icon phonebook. This would show an up and down arrow so as to scroll up and down to the required number. Next was to scroll up or down to the required number. The last step is just pick up the handset and the phone would dial automatically. It did not matter how many times we did this, she just could not master this simple operation. She would read the first step, and nod her head as if to say she got it. Then she would go to the second step, but within a second or two the first step was already lost, and so there was no context to understand what it was from. And so, even as simple as it is, the automatic telephone book is not being used, and probably never will be.

This, according to the books, is a classic mid-term dementia symptom, where things stored in the short term memory are gone within thirty seconds. It is also the reason why Dad looks at his watch thirty times an hour – because there is no recollection of the last viewing within his short term memory.

Typically, in people without dementia, events, such as reading about the telephone book instructions in a modern phone or taking in the time after looking at a watch are stored in the short-term memory box. From there, they are passed into the longer-term memory box. But if the short-term memory box is emptied before its contents are passed to the longer-term memory box then there is nothing to pass on.

That is also the reason why in many people, with one of the many dementia types, they have good long-term memory. The reason for this is because the longer-term memories are already firmly stored in the long-term memory box. That is why Helen, even with this problem, still possess great general knowledge.

22nd June

Off to Dad again, but today we had an appointment with a lady who worked for the hospital, and looks after the facilitation of the elderly who end up in hospital.

As we drove, I heard, "About twenty years ago there was a fire along this section that totally devastated the bush. It was so bad that there was only dirt left. Houses were lost. It was terrible. But it amazes me that it has recovered as it has. Nature it truly wonderful".

'Fuck' I think, but say, "Yes indeed it is". Well her words may not have been exactly the same but I am sure you get the drift. And so as not to annoy you, I can say that we did that trip about thirty times, and sixty times (both ways) I heard about twenty years ago there was a...

Dad's story

Dad was in France at the outbreak of the war. All my life I had been itching to know his story of that time. But, always vague and contradictory, it was hard to know fact from fiction, lie or truth.

The following is the story he told us.

Lech Grundkowski (Dad, Lou) was born in 1922 in Poland and lived in Bromberg. Many of the residence held allegiance with Germany as the following outline shows.

The area had previously been known as Bydgoszcz but in 1772 and was annexed by the Kingdom of Prussia (Prussia was a loose alliance of states that made up most of the Germanic Empire) and renamed Bromberg.

In 1910 the city had 57,700 inhabitants of which eighty-four percent were Germans and sixteen percent Poles. This was the populous that Dads parents would have lived in and I can understand from this why his family had an allegiance to Germany.

In 1919 the city was assigned to newly sovereign Poland (through the Paris Peace Conference and the Versailles Treaty). As a result, the local populace were required to acquire Polish citizenship or leave the country. This led to a steady and significant decline of ethnic Germans. However, the German culture and ethnicity was well entrenched and the amendment of laws may not have changed as much as many of the residents believed in the structure. Dad was fluent in German, had marginal Polish, and later French.

From what I can gather, Dad had a fairly happy upbringing there. But Dad has never been one to give information and so the few scanty facts that I give on the following lines have been plucked together with great difficulty, but also from Shayne (my ex-wife who has done the family tree on my side), and a friend called Marcel.

Dad had a younger brother called Zenon, of whom I shall give you a bit about later on.

The Grundkowski family moved to France in around 1929, so Dad was about seven years of age. Dad's father was French and, we believe, a fitter and turner by trade and also a musician. They went to France to find work, as apparently in that time in Poland there was very little.

They lived in a small industrial town, Imphy in the Nievre region, on the Loire River, which is pretty much right in the middle of France. It

OH HELL

was here that my grandfather played music at night and worked in a factory in the day. It was also here, in this factory, where Dad gained his first work experience and probably his first experience on a metal lath.

The other day I asked him how old was he when he started work and he said sixteen. But when I asked him the next day he said he was fourteen. I would think fourteen was more likely. Later on I found a document that showed indenture papers.

By all reports this was the best time of Dad's youth, and when he did talk about it, it was with great fondness. He played soccer and also was a cyclist and raced in some bike races. Apparently his father wanted Dad to also be a musician but Dad had no inclination and seemingly no talent.

However, this happy life came to an abrupt end in 1940 when the German war machine overran France. The Germans, always wanting to feed that hungry machine with new troops, rounded up all the young men and gave them an ultimatum: either you fight for us or you die.

Well this is the story Dad often told. He said there was no decision and so most were recruited. But I doubt that he wanted to go to war, nor to fight (not many did), I do believe that he was loyal and respected Germany. I also believe that he would believe in their cause. I say this because as a child growing up in his household, whenever he spoke of Germany, it was almost with reverence. Of course, whenever he did, invariably he was drunk. And yes, he was drunk on most weekends from Friday evening until Sunday evening. He also spoke with hate about certain races, especially the Jews, and was probably indoctrinated by the Nazi rhetoric. Later, I was to learn that Dad, and the entire family were pro the German cause, and Zenon was a member of the Nazi Youth Brigade. Even as a child, his dislike for other races did not sit well with me and somehow I knew that it was wrong to hate a race as much has he seemed to.

Now to enlist in the German army, said Dad, he found himself repatriated to Germany where he underwent some sort of basic training and found himself in the engineering unit, whereby he helped look after trucks and machinery. It would seem at this stage that he had found his forte because this is what he was very good at.

However, Shayne and I started researching public records. The following comments sets the background to much of the German recruiting efforts.

On 1st September 1939 World War II began with the German attack of Poland. Germany, in need of manpower had a programme of conscription. To supplement this, all captured prisoners of war were put to work. But even so, there was still a massive shortfall for the German Armed Forces and the rapidly growing demand of manpower of the German war industry.

Forced Labour in the National Socialist State as taken from the following site:

http://www.bundesarchiv.de/zwangsarbeit/index.html.en

Behind the approaching troops the Federal Labour Institutions immediately began erecting their service offices in order to recruit foreign workers to work as volunteers or bring them by force to Germany in cooperation with the "Reichssicherheitshauptamt" and the German economy.

More than twelve million women and men from all across Europe who suffered severe deprivation of their rights by regulations and contractual conditions, fooled by false promises, accommodated in poor barracks and camps, malnourished and held back from returning to their home countries worked in all parts of the German Reich. Abused as human material for the production in the defence industry as well as in agriculture and in public utility operations they became forced labourers of the Germans.

Most of them came from Poland, Belarus, Russia and Ukraine.

After the rapid capture of the Netherlands, Belgium and France in spring and summer 1940, many POWs from Belgium (approximately

65,000) and France (approximately 1.3 million) were made available to the German defence industry and agriculture.

http://www.bundesarchiv.de/zwangsarbeit/geschichte/auslaendisch/freiwillige/index.html.en

Belgium and The Netherlands

While the Commissioner of the Reich for the Netherlands kept tightening the compulsory measures with respect to the deployment from February 1941 until autumn 1944, the occupying forces in Belgium and France were primarily relying on willing workers volunteering for work. In June 1940 it was agreed with the Belgium authorities that Belgians were not to be forced to work in Germany and that volunteers were not to be deployed in the defence industry, an agreement the German administration only adhered to until 1942. That way some 189,000 Belgians went to Germany volunteering for a compulsory employment.

A year later the obligation to work was introduced. Now every male between eighteen and fifty years and every unmarried woman between twenty-one (later eighteen) and thirty-five years could be conscripted to work in the German Reich. Finally complete, birth cohorts were obligated to work. The number of Belgians working in the Reich during World War II was around 375,000, the number of Dutch people was around 475,000.

France

Recruitment office for French workers in Paris, February 1943

(Source: Federal Archives, Bild 183-2002-0225-500)

In occupied France a great number of men were quickly and violently forced to join the Organisation Todt and subsequently deployed in Northern France. The German occupying forces were initially (mainly) relying on volunteers.

In the spring of 1942 some 845,000 Frenchmen were working for the Organisation Todt, the German Armed Forces and the defence industry within France. At that point in time the German labour policy towards France saw a fundamental change. In September 1942 work became obligatory for all men and women here as well. In order to obtain the workforce ordered by the Reich, the Service du Travail Obligatoire (STO) was established, which placed the required manpower into Germany by conscription of entire birth cohorts, which was by no means on a voluntary basis. Merely as part of the agreed actual and apparent exchange of POWs against civil workers, at least 390,000 French civil workers, amongst them numerous skilled workers, entered the Reich until 1943. The number of POWs, however, declined rather insignificantly through releases and returns home, more so by transfers into a civil status or deceases. The total number of French civil workers throughout the entire war was slightly more than 1 million people.

The following speech was given by Fritz Sauckel, Chief Representative for the Deployment of Labour, speaking to advisors and Leaders of Deployment of Labour in Paris on 18 March 1944;

"I would seriously like to draw your attention to the following, my dear deployment officers: The "Führer" expects from us and I expect from you that human transports keep rolling. From now on your work will be assessed according to the number of thousands of workers entering the Reich every day, since the Reich needs them."

However, the status of Western European workers was still significantly different to that of the workers from the East, namely the Poles and Czechs. They were generally better accommodated and fed, they were paid better and had to adhere to regulations, which were a lot less harsh with respect to the interaction with Germans. The causes for the betterment of Dutch, Belgians and Frenchmen was both in the National Socialist racial ideology, according to which these nations were of higher rank but even more in the centuries old, traditionally rooted conceptional pattern and empathies towards these nations within the general German public. Nevertheless, they did not reach as far as completely ruling out any discriminations and special regulations. The longer the war lasted, the more the forceful character of these employment relationships became evident.

So based on the above, and if one was to believe what Dad said, which would have been that he went the Service du Travail Obligatoire (STO) method, it would look like he was forced into labour.

But, by Dad's own admission, he was in the German army (and I have photos of him in a uniform), plus with what Marcel told us – so this is clearly a contradiction.

June 21 – Smiley

Off to Bernie this morning to meet with the Aged Care liaison officer, to discuss Dad's case. As you may have realised in these few early pages I do not call most people in any organisation by their correct name. I do this out of respect for them and also because I cannot afford the litigation. I will call this person Smiley because of her wonderfully positive attitude, she always seemed to smile. Short, plump, more elderly than young, she was a sweetie.

The outcome of the appointment with Smiley was good one.

This appointment was not only about Dad but also Helen. In relation to Dad her concern was that the longer term treatment would be ongoing and that she will try to get him out of the hospital and into an aged care facility. She felt that he was ready at this point in time to make that move. But as I learnt, it is not so easy to just to get someone into an aged care facility as there are more elderly than there are places, rooms and beds – someone has to die first. Smiley said, "I will phone all the facilities in the Devonport area every couple of days to see if someone had", as she euphemistically call it, "moved on, from which to offer the new space".

Her concern with Helen is because of her history of anxiety and suicide attempt. Smiley felt that Helen was on the edge of decline and could spiral down very quickly. She wanted to know who I was, and who was looking after Helen. She made some suggestions in terms of getting different organisations involved.

Another question Smiley asked was, "Is Helen still driving?" When I said "Yes", she said that will probably fall away fairly soon. Of course I want to support Helen and keep her driving for as long as possible, for without a license, and once I float on to where ever I go next, her independence will be severely curtailed. Smiley was adamant, saying that she felt that Helen's reflexes in the event of a potential accident would not be good enough, and that she could hurt people.

I disagreed and said that mostly Helen's reflexes are good, But Smiley honed in to that word 'mostly' and countered with "And what happened when her reflexes are not working on a given day?"

I guess her argument is right. However, I also feel that there are many people whose reflexes are not good because they are tied, focusing on their mobile phone, screaming children, daydreaming, intoxicated, et cetera. I think the most important thing for Helen with her driving is that she understands when not to drive. Certainly whilst I am about, there is no reason for her to drive when she is tired or stressed. When I am gone she will have to have more discipline. But there is another thing as well; when Dad is in the care facility, and only five minutes up the road, Helen's driving will be localised – that is to the shops, which are only a few kilometres away, or up to see Dad or around town on errands.

All in all, I think Smiley's support is very good and I'm happy to have it.

Dad was much the same as yesterday, but the nursing staff said that once the meds take hold he will be more compus mentus.

I think it would be easier to have ten hours of chopping down trees, than one hour of sitting with Dad. Such was the stress of it all.

OH HELL
More on Dad's history

Shayne, through her genealogy discovered a childhood school friend of Zenon's. This was in Imphy, where Dad's given history was disputable. This man is a French citizen and asked me not to name him in this book. I am grateful for the information he gave us, over many emails, where, either in halting English, or French (which I would run through an on-line translating programme), offered much plausible information. I shall call him Marcel.

Marcel was younger than Dad, having been born in 1929, but remembered Dad from *'our children's games'* in Imphy. Imphy, Marcel explained, is a little town with many factories in Nièvre (France).

Marcel had been trying to contact his long lost friend (Zenon), who he had not seen since the war and so went on line to see what he could find. When he found Shayne's family tree he contacted her.

The following has been pieced together from those emails from Marcel.

After Dad's family relocated to France, and specifically Imphy, Zenon befriended Marcel as they were in the same school and were the same age. Through Zenon, and by virtue that Imphy was a relatively small town, Marcel got to know the family. He wrote; Your father's father played violin and was a teacher but he also worked in a factory. Your father's mother was a pretty blond woman, who also played guitar and sang.

But when talking about Dad, he wrote:

Lech left France with his father as volunteers to work in Germany in 1942 or 1943 (an intriguing piece of information).

Zenon and his mother remained in France.

If what Marcel says is true, there is a gross contradiction to what Dad told us that because France was overrun by the Germans, and at virtual gunpoint was forced into the German army. That did happen, especially through the Organisation Todt. But if what Marcel said is true; that Dad left France to go and work in Germany in 1942. By this time the war was well underway. I have no reason to doubt the truthfulness of Marcel's information or his memory. However, it does not make sense as to why they would willingly go to Germany to offer service. What it further indicates, is that Dad's sympathies lay with the German cause, and that the helping of that cause was a better option than staying in France and taking his chances. Yet, he must have realised that if he returned home, that he could have been shot as a collaborator by the French underground. And lastly on this; remember Dad hated France and had bad memories of the French who bullied him at school. Perhaps the German war machine was his escape, or his revenge.

Irrespective of this being true or not, I can understand why Dad propagated the story of him being forced into the German army. For instance, if he had been caught, or freed by the Americans, it would have been pragmatic for him to say that, as if it was known that he was a volunteer in the German army then his treatment may have been different. There are just too many unknowns in this time.

Nevertheless, Dad was in the German army and trained in Germany. We do not know anything about his early years of the war, other than the fact that he was trained in mechanics and worked to keep army vehicles running. Nor do we know where he may have served.

But later, we do know that he was sent to Stalingrad in Russia. Russia was Hitler's biggest mistake and many historians say this was the turning point in the war. Hitler ignored the warnings of his closest advisers, and also history; as Napoleon also failed to conquer Russia. Russia is too far away, too large and the winters too severe. Supply lines were always going to be difficult, and that proved to be the case for that German campaign. There was another reason why the Germans were defeated in Russia, and that is that they attacked a year too late as at that time Russia would have been ill prepared. But Russia is the largest country in the world and has a massive population, and so when they threw everything that they had into preparing armament and defences, and with literally millions of troops at their disposal, they threw it all at the Germans.

OH HELL

Hitler had Stalingrad attacked in 1942 but after five months of fighting and the gaining of some Russian territory, the Russians started their counter offensive and became dominant. This battle is often regarded as the bloodiest and most brutal campaign in the history of warfare. This is some claim as we humans have been pretty gruesome over the centuries.

Although the military leaders asked, then implored Hitler to give the command to retreat, he forbade any sort of retreat. Not only that, he ordered the commanders to fight to the last man, to the last bullet, and that those men who were sacrificing their life would do so and be enshrined forever. Doubt if Dad agrees with this sentiment.

However, the situation was so bad that a shambled retreat occurred anyway, in the end 91,000 troops were caught or surrendered to the Russians.

There were a small number who escaped the Russian clutches, perhaps 5,000. Out of these, a few hundred, mainly officers, or those who had money, bribed the pilots of the aircraft's to fly them out. Apparently there was pandemonium with people kicking and fighting to get onto those planes because there was no organised transport. The rest walked the 2000 km back to Germany, which for most represented death.

Dad does not talk, or never did, as to how he survived and what actually happened to him. It would seem to me that there was one of two scenarios. The first was that he was one of those who walked the 2000 km back to Germany, through that freezing winter, surviving on the bodies of the troops who died in the fight on the way into Russia.

The second possible scenario is that he was one of the troops that ultimately surrendered to the Russians. In which case he would have been in a prisoner of war in one of the infamous Gulags (prisoner of war camp) there. The conditions in the Gulags were grim beyond grim. Food and water were always in short supply. Many were shot or mutilated, and most starved to death or died of disease. Those that lived were used as slave labour where they were beaten to continue working. Even when the war was over, the Russians retained (against international convention) many of the Germans as they needed the labour. Most simply disappeared.

Dad was in a prisoner of war camp. I learnt this from his hospital records. They could only have got this information from Dad or Helen. If it was Dad, then it is likely that he gave this information to his medical practitioner when he was much younger. If it was Helen, then she knows more than she thinks she does.

If he had been a POW – where? In Russia, or after walking back to Germany, caught by the Brits or the Americans? My guess is that he walked back and was caught by the US troops. Either way, it would have been horrific but far worse if it was with the Russians. It also shows an incredible sense of stubborn survival. This is playing out in his current situation. You have got to admire those traits.

If he was caught by the US troops, I believe that he would have told them that he was forced to support the Germans through the Organisation Todt. Clearly they believed him.

It was in 1949 when Dad immigrated to Australia, he did so with his young wife, Hildegard. They were transported from Italy on the USS General Omar Bundy a Squier-class transport ship for the U.S. Navy. The passenger list was almost exclusively refugees or displaced persons.

The following is from an immigration document pertaining to his arrival and status:

>International Refugee Organisation
>
>Group Resettlement to Australia

This passenger list contains individuals and families that migrated to Australia after World War II from various European Countries including Germany, Hungary, Russia, Ukraine, Latvia, Poland,

Czechoslovakia, Romania, etc. Most passengers are World War II refugees or displaced persons. Dad's name was on that list.

Before leaving for Australia they were in an Italian refugee camp called Bagnoli. Dad never said anything about this.

Hildegard became my mother. They wanted to get away from the madness of Europe, to try and put it all behind them. But how could they? Those horrific memories would have been etched into every brain cell. Little movies of slaughter would have automatically played in the mind whenever a trigger would set it off. And the fear, how does one escape the memory of being in such fear? I always said my Dad's head was 'not right', but is there any way that after what he went through that it could be right? Those demons had him all of his days. They still haunt him as can be seen in his response and behaviour to the carers of the nursing home, where he panics if touched, especially by a male carer in their work cloths, which to him may look like uniforms. There is such fear in his response, his face tells all.

In the care facility, they all know his record and say that his behaviour is consistent with those of similar war history. There are many in the facility who are also in their nineties, who also served in one army or another in that brutal war, and most act in similar ways.

22nd June

Not a good decision to let Helen drive today as she drove like she was in a dream. I took over and as she continued her dream I allowed my thoughts to wonder. Perhaps Smiley is right. I will have to learn to recognise when she will not be on top of it.

Because we were heading towards Dad, that's where my thoughts went and as they did they went to places that they had not wandered to for a long time.

There were two events, both similar in some ways. The first one was where I remembered being woken up, it was early and still dark. I must have been about eight years old. Although still half asleep I was half dragged and carried to the car were I continued my half-awake half-sleep dosing. But as the light came and the distance became shorter to our destination I felt happiness with what was to come. And then we arrived at Bobin Head where Mum and Dad had hired a row boat. It was not long before the five of us were far from the wharf and way down the waterway. The weather was one of those perfect Sydney spring days, the deep blue of the sky contrasted with the emerald green of the water. Distant head lands, perfect crisp jewels, gave form to the waterway – all clean, as if just unwrapped. Being the lightest, I always sat in that little seat in the bow. Sometimes I would turn my body around to see the way that we were going or sit facing backwards and watch Dad's back as he pulled the oars. As a family we tended not to talk a lot, and so I was entranced with his back and forth rhythm, arms in perfect time to his body-rhythm. And each time the oars hit the water in front of Dad, there was a light splash and swirling of water, until the oars were behind him, towards me. With the rhythm and the sound I would be mesmerised and could sit watching for hours.

Days like these happened occasionally, not often enough to forge a relationship with him.

We would get to a spot where he felt that the fish may bite. Sometimes they did, sometimes they didn't. We would all throw our lines, but before I did he said, "Let me help you tie on your hook. Now watch closely" as he threaded the line through the hook, made the loop, and wrapped it around about eight times to pull it tight and firm. He would pass the bait to me as I was to put my own bait on. And then over the side the line and the bait would go and I would fish, like the rest of them, I thought. Seldom did I catch anything, but that did not matter, as the gentle rocking of the boat soothed, as did the early morning sun. If someone said anything Dad would loud-

OH HELL

ly whisper, "shoosh! The fish will hear you and run away." I always thought this funny and wondered if fish had ears? I never saw any ears on the fish that had been pulled, except for that small stingray that John pulled in – where the wings look like big ears.

As I drove towards the hospital, I reflected that one of the reasons why these outings were more relaxed was because he was more of a participant, as opposed to the periphery, which is what he normally was. Fishing was his love, it softened him and he was far more relaxed and we were allowed to join in.

The second event was one where I also was told to focus, like I had to when he showed me how to tie the hook, but this one had a different outcome. His intent was very different.

It was a Friday night and he was more jovial than he would normally be. Yes sure, his joviality as you will see, is likely to be different from yours or mine. By this time he had been drinking about two hours and was in that merriment stage, whereby he was more relaxed but not yet totally in the inebriated stage that he would be later on as he got deeper into the weekend. I used to recognise this merriment stage as it was a precursor to the belligerent and sour stage that he would get into, when every single cell of his body was at maximum alcohol saturation. In this merriment stage he moved out of his normal sullen state and was talkative.

I do not know why this particular Friday night was different to others but there was champagne to be had. I seem to remember that we had guests, but cannot remember who or how many. He asked me if I would like to see how to open up a bottle of champagne. I had never seen champagne before and so said yes. He came to me, very close and bent down, and said "You have to watch very closely otherwise you will miss it". At this, he placed the bottle only about 100 mm away from my forehead, pointing towards my face, and started to use his thumbs to pry off the cork. Watch closely he encouraged "… it's coming soon … it won't be long…" as his thumbs continued to work the cork... The next thing I was on my back on the floor with an aching forehead, such was the force of the cork as its pressure hit me. I was stunned, hurt and embarrassed and lay on the floor. He was bent over in hysterics, such was his perverse sense of humour.

Had I been hit with a cricket ball on the head I am not sure if I would have been any more hurt, such was the force and the hardness of that champagne cork.

As I'm driving towards him in his hospital bed I shake my head and cannot understand why he would think that doing this to his eight-year-old child is fun.

23rd June

Not much happened today. But my pen 'played'. This is what it came up with.

I'm sixty-four, and most in this institution would consider me young. However, to the young, I have reached old. But to me I am still young inside – an old man only on the outside.

Chocolate, consumed often, taste just as great now as it did when I was eleven years old. And the eruptions of laughter are just as raucous as my fifteen-year-old self was.

But it's the dreams that keep me young inside. Mine are still vigorous and probably unrealistic, which is good, as we must reach high with our dreams. They come in waves that refresh my being. They may not be dreams where, triumphantly I am receiving pats on the back after scoring the winning goal, as my twelve year old self would have had. But the eagerness is ever present and springs forth with power and without provocation.

Surely, it's our dreams that keep our spirit strong within? Perhaps we start to die when the dreams become fewer.

The child-like need of the two-year-old's independence is scaffold in my psychic – leave me to do it. Nor am I locked into the past, with a blanket on my knee, it is the future that occupies my mind – of wanderlust and things to create and do. Many my age are already retired – bullshit, no way.

Until the end of my life I will be pregnant with dreams, plans and accomplishments, as really that's how we are built. Where the mind is willing to go, the body will somehow follow. And as there is evolution of all life, there is still evolution within me – nothing stagnant here. New things to learn, mistakes to make, embarrassments to be had. All embraced with glee.

24th June

We needed to get a handle on Helen's mental condition and I made an appointment with her doctor for a pre-dementia examination. This is a basic test that the nurse does that indicates if there could be dementia. Helen passed this with flying colours, meaning that this highly intelligent person only scored 28%. Twenty years ago she is likely to have scored 100% in no time.

The result did not prove anything that we did not know. But now that the medical institution acknowledges her problem we can pursue it further to see how advanced she is, and more importantly if there are any programmes that she can go on to slow the process down.

The next step is to see a psychologist for a fuller investigation. That appointment has been set for about a month's time.

28th June

When Helen had her suicide attempt, as part of her recovery programme she was to see a psychologist. Well, there were a bunch of them and in most instances it was just going through the motions for Helen. But on her own, she found a psychologist who she liked and who she felt helped her. I shall call this psychologist, 'Shrink'.

Helen had been going to Shrink about every two months. This was not only to be counselled, but also to renew her prescription for various anti-depressants. The main one that Shrink seemed to settle on was Lomac20.

The other day we received a call from Shrink asking if Helen is she was Okay as she had an appointment last week but missed it. The new appointment was for today. Helen asked me if I would attend with her so I can remember what may need to be remembered and also to bring up any issues over the last month that may be relevant.

Most of the appointment went as expected, but I felt that I needed to tell Shrink about the dementia assessment and the results. For a moment Shrink was quiet as she seemed to be thinking. But when she spoke, it was with a considered tone that was directed to Helen, "I do not believe that you have dementia... I think all your issues are stressed related. Once you remove the stress, things should improve".

If she is right, then it would make a massive difference to Helen's longevity, as most forms of dementia, being a disease, ultimately lead to death.

Sadly, Helen forgot this and I had to remind her several times that night – "Shrink believes you do not have dementia and she feels you can recover".

9th July

Another appointment with Smiley. She informed me that they were preparing to move Dad to another aged care facility that had a spare bed. Apparently the bed was in the room of another patient and the idea was that they would put him in there until such time as a single room became available. This did not seem to be such a good idea

OH HELL

but we were willing to go along with it as we wanted him in a better facility.

Sometime later I spoke to one of the nurses in charge of the ward that Dad was in, and I asked her if it would be possible for Helen to travel in the patient transport vehicle with Dad? "No" was the reply, because sometimes they transport other patients. Okay, I said, but what about sedation? She replied that there would either be no sedation or a very minor one. I thought this okay because I wanted Dad to be aware of what was happening as I felt he would be in better control. I managed to find out when he was being transported and so we would arrange to be at the aged care facility to meet Dad.

That afternoon we went to the facility, after making an appointment, to check it out. It looked great. Although we were not entirely happy with the fact that that he would be sharing room – we know that Dad is not always the most pleasant company. Nevertheless, it could not be helped and so we did not push the issue, especially knowing that they did not have another room available. Someone had to die first.

We were being shown around the facility by one of the management staff who was friendly and helpful. At one stage we entered a room, which was quite large, like a small hall. In it were about fifteen residents, all seated, most with rugs across their laps. Out of the fifteen, twelve would have been asleep and the other three seem to be dozing but with their eyes open. The scene was so still, it could have been a painting. Our guide happily informed us that this is the activity room. Yes, I can be crass and had a mental giggle.

Back to her office, where we were given reams of forms to take home and fill out. Australia is the land of bureaucracy and certainly this was living up to her title with the number of forms and the variety. We Australian's are a creative bunch, as the forms covered a myriad of back-side covering scenarios. Armed with these we took them home to work through, one by one. Of course this is what we did, but the worst part was probably the duplication or triplication or even fourthlication if there is such a word. Ho hum…

Today we have a new stove to cook on. The other day I went into the garage and saw a brand-new stove. Wondering about this I went and asked Helen. For a time there was a blank look and then as the light dawned she smiled and said, "Yes, I bought that but forgot about it". Later when I saw the documentation for the stove it had been purchased some ten months earlier. I phoned a few electricians and got quotes to install it and today the selected electrician did the job.

10th July

Today was the day. The patient transport was to pick Dad up at about 10:30 this morning and so I arranged for Helen and I to be at the facility well in advance of its arriving. When it did we met the trolley that Dad was on, he was asleep, very deeply asleep. We followed the trolley into the room, and met the other man, whom I shall call Freddie.

The paramedics organised Dad and put him into his new bed. We were amazed at how deeply asleep he was. It was then that I realised that he was more than just sedated, he was anaesthetised and totally comatose. This was most unfortunate.

We sat with Dad for about four hours and not once did he move, as if a marble figure. But after four hours we had other things that we had to do and so we left. It would seem that it was not long after we left that he started to revive. At that time a male orderly woke him to take him to the toilet. This was not a good move, as I shall explain in a few minutes. What also made it worse was that Dad was so totally disorientated – like going to sleep in Hong Kong and waking up in the rainforests of Brazil. All the faces were new and Helen was nowhere to be seen.

Helen and I suspect that as a result of his being in a POW camp in the Second World War that he is likely to have been mistreated by the guards (orderlies and guards would be much the same in his mind)) and that he had a flashback and reacted badly. With his disorientation and fear, he was scared and irrational. He shouted, kicked and lashed out at everyone who went near him. Apparently this went on for a couple of hours until they phoned me and said they were going to send Dad back to Burnie as he was disrupting the other patients.

Without him knowing it, with all he had been through, it is probable that he would have had Post Traumatic Stress Syndrome. In those days, they did not recognise the disease or treat it and after the war millions of others were let loose back into society with traumatised minds.

The following comes from the Beyond Blue website:

People with Traumatic Stress Syndrome often experience feelings of panic or extreme fear, similar to the fear they felt during the traumatic event.

A person with Post Traumatic Stress Syndrome experiences four main types of difficulties.

Re-living the traumatic event – The person relives the event through unwanted and recurring memories, often in the form of vivid images and nightmares. There may be intense emotional or physical reactions, such as sweating, heart palpitations or panic when reminded of the event.

Being overly alert or wound up – The person experiences sleeping difficulties, irritability and lack of concentration, becoming easily startled and constantly on the lookout for signs of danger.

Avoiding reminders of the event – The person deliberately avoids activities, places, people, thoughts or feelings associated with the event because they bring back painful memories.

Feeling emotionally numb – The person loses interest in day-to-day activities, feels cut off and detached from friends and family, or feels emotionally flat and numb.

Without a doubt Dad had many of these symptoms so it is likely that his demented mind returned to those horrible times, and so of course he lashed out.

We could not believe this development and were most annoyed. Into the car we climbed and went to the facility as fast as we could. When we got there he was not in the room that he had been allocated but was in the activity room (all the other patients were in their rooms and probably in bed) away from the other patient so as not to disturb him. When we found him there, there was a lovely carer who was sitting with him, holding his hand and trying to support him in the process. We could see how gentle and supportive she was. Upon seeing us she stood up, where she and I stepped away from the bed to chat, whilst Helen went to try and placate Dad.

Literally the first thing this lovely lady said was that it was out of her hands and that the order was given to send Dad back by management as they can't afford to disrupt the other guests. I could understand this but felt that they could have tried a little bit longer and said, "Perhaps they should have phoned us earlier, because look, he's already calming down with Helen's attention", which is what we originally wanted. I then asked her if the order to return him could be cancelled, as now he's much quieter.

I could see that she really wanted to help us and she said that she would go and phone management. And so she slipped away to do so. Three or four minutes later she returned and straight away I could see that she was unable to change the mind of the manager. Her gaze was downcast nodding "No". The manager in charge said they just can't take the risk of residents being distracted anymore.

At this, Helen became King Kong like. She stood up from the bed, far taller and stronger than her normal diminutive self and in a voice that quivered with anguish but with immense determination said, "This man is my husband and he is ninety-two years old, how dare you shunt him back and forth like a sack of potatoes?"

The poor carer did not know what to say and could only agree with Helen. It was not her fault and if she had her way then Dad would have stayed. I then reiterated how badly the entire transfer had been managed but of course this was all to no avail. The transporter returned at about 11 PM, but this time I virtually pushed Helen onto the paramedics to make sure that she went in the transporter with him to try and keep him as calm as possible. I then followed them in our car back to Burnie hospital.

Helen stayed with him as he was readmitted into Emergency, and until he was back in his ward. This time it was to another ward. Finally he settled down and went to sleep. We then drove home, arriving about 2AM.

OH HELL
11th July

Downcast, we were having breakfast when my phone rang. It was the manager of the facility who had phoned to apologise for the way things turned out last night. It would seem that that nice carer had related all that we said, especially the appalling management of the process. She was sympathetic but said that they could not have kept Dad there any longer in case he did disrupt the other residents. I then asked her if we could make an appointment and I would see her later that morning.

At the time of the appointment it was obvious that they had had some sort of change of mind and that they were keen for Dad to return. So what was suggested; now that he is back at Burnie, that the hospital stabilise him over the next week and then the facility would look at bringing him back again. Their attitude was most sympathetic and compassionate and really wanted to help Dad and Helen. So even though we had had a tumultuous start with the facility I liked it and felt comfortable that it would ultimately work out okay.

This morning my phone started beeping at me, the bit that says my battery is almost flat. I went to get my charger, which had been sitting on a dining room chair, next to where I set up my little office, but it was gone. I searched everywhere, the phone shut itself off and I sat down frustrated. Upon coming into the room I asked Helen if she had seen it, "No" was her answer. Of course that did not mean anything. Later on, as we sat down for lunch I asked again, "Was it black and about two feet long?" she asked.

"Yes that's it."

"Yes I threw it out. When I saw it I wondered what it was, and came to the conclusion that it was not needed."

"Is it in the garbage", I asked.

"Yes, but that was yesterday and the garbage was taken away today."

Damn, I thought to myself, as I grab the car keys to drive into town to buy another one.

12th July

We had an appointment at the hospital for the purpose of planning Dad's third removal from the hospital, back to the aged care facility.

As per normal I let Helen drive on the way there. But today we needed to pull over and I took over, it was as if her mind was still back at home in bed. As mentioned, I do want her to drive as long as possible, and so this is a bit of a blow. But to soften it, I suggest that we pull into a fish and chip shop in Ulverstone and have fish and chips for lunch, and I take over from there.

Once we had our lunch we drove around the river, about half a kilometre, and parked facing the river, under some willows. Fortunately for our amusement workers were building a pier and so we watched them as they inserted a pylon. This was most interesting, as it was done with various sleeves where one would fit inside the previous sleeve. Each time one was inserted, a large crane with a weight would thump it down into the ground under the water. It must have been muddy and soft because with each thump it would go down about half a meter.

So interesting was this to us, that on another trip we veered around to this point to see how far they had developed the pier. However, as if that day was for our own amusement, there had not been any more work done and the site seemed to be locked up.

The meeting with Smiley, the Aged Care Facility lady, the manager of the nursing home, and a doctor, yes, another, went well. Sounds crazy, but not only did they listen to my requests they accepted them; that Helen be allowed to accompany Dad in the transporter; that he be given only the mildest of sedatives; that it be around 11:00am as he was normally more conscious and aware by then; and of course that he had his own room. Lastly, that Helen be allowed to stay in the room with him continuously until Dad settled, be that a day, week or month.

The move was to happen in two days' time.

We had a meltdown tonight. I think Helen is stressed from the tension of the day, and continues being worn down from the daily trips back and forth, as I mentioned before, the round trip was about three hours. The meltdown came about dinner time, with the hand wringing of the handkerchief, hunched over, tears and snot. "Oh why is he like this… I wish I could do more… I wish he would die… I wish I was dead."

"Come Helen, sit down and I'll make you a cup of tea."

Black, weak and two sugars is how she likes it. As she sipped she settled and felt a bit better. We spoke about the hospital and hoped that it would be better when he was in the aged nursing facility.

She turned to look at me and said, "Thank you, you have been most kind…" Then she burst out into more crying "…you know, no one has ever supported me as much as you have. Thank you".

I was stunned and saddened. Surely she did not have to wait for seventy-three years for a family member to support her?

When she said this, it was with a smile. There was a time where she smiled often, but in these grim times it seldom appeared. The smile, when there, is rich, generous and draws you in, a reflection of a happier time.

13th July

This was the day Dad was moved back to the facility. Helen was a mess before we started. But I knew she would be able to pull herself together and powerfully present herself for the event. This time it all went smoothly because of the way we had organised it.

We got to Burnie hospital well in time and Dad was awake and moderately lucid. The head nurse came in and gave him that light sedative, and it was not long before the paramedics came to transport him. Helen was with him the whole time, holding his hand. Into the back of the transporter she went and all was fine. I drove behind them and so arrived at the same time.

When he arrived they were waiting for him, and within about two minutes he was in his new room. It had a large window that opened onto a courtyard and let the winter sun in. Outside the window was a bush that softened the area with greenery, a nice room I thought. But I also thought that this is the room that he had come to die in.

As per the arrangement, they moved a second bed into the room for Helen and that is where she stayed for about a forty-eight hour period. He was mostly fine throughout this time, with the door closed he was not nearly as disruptive as he was a previous time.

When Helen finally returned home she was totally drained and fell asleep on the couch. When she woke up she was stressed and dysfunctional. But she had done what she needed to do and that was all that mattered.

14th July

Today we have an appointment with a Geriatrician. Isn't that a lovely word? A Geriatrician is a psychologist who looks after old people.

OH HELL

This one is in Hobart, so I took the wheel for this extended trip.

It was a good appointment, as it was the full assessment to determine if Helen has dementia.

After the tests, although she did not score well, he does not believe she has dementia and thinks that her issues are stress related. This is really good news, because as mentioned earlier, there is only one final result with dementia and Alzheimer's, and that is death, not to forget it is strewn with horrific difficulties along the way. What this means, if he is correct – then there is a possible path to recuperation for her.

To prove his suspicion, he has booked her an MRI scan in a couple weeks' time. With both dementia and Alzheimer's, plaque (called beta amyloid) is formed. This plaque is a protein, which has no use and damages or kills the neurons within the brain. The MRI should show evidence of the plaque. Of course we hope not to see any.

His opinion is such a positive thing and gives a real hope. We look forward to the MRI as categorical proof for her.

There is another reason why it is such good news and that is; I now do not have to continue studying these diseases!

Still the path will be not be easy, and the main stress of her husband dying is still to be overcome, and until such time as Dad goes there will be no respite. Once all that does happen, and it is over, then with a bit of luck she may settle down and some of her faculties return. I do not know how long this process will take and must remain here until it is all settled.

Five minutes later though, she has forgotten this news. I tell her at least six times that night.

"And what is the MRI for?" she keeps asking.

15th July

As part of the process to get Dad into the nursing care facility, we have to have a doctor who would take him on as a permanent patient. Easy I thought, I shall make a few phone calls and organise. No, it did not work out this way as there are a shortage of doctors in the area. Some have moved away, some had become pregnant, others had retired, and some that I found out would not treat patients in the nursing home because there is not enough money in it. Of course this last statement was not told to me directly, but after some digging I found out that most of these suburban surgeries are owned and run by companies. Of course they have bean counters (accountants). Bean counters are tasked with counting lots of beans. They have an inherent need to be able to count more beans this month than they did last month. And if they don't they get fired. So they have instructed the doctors of their surgeries not to care for the elderly in facilities as the 'time to patient' ratio does not optimise the value proposition. Sorry about the business speak but it is true.

When speaking to some of the doctors, and trying to do my best selling job, I had to revert to the odd fib and tell them that Dad is a nice, gentle and quite old man who would happily receive them. I am not sure if crossing my fingers behind my back will save me from going to hell when I die, but for goodness sake, I needed a doctor for my old man. And when I would say things to them, such as; "please doctor, this is not a long-term case. Can you not take him on knowing that he is not likely to be around in another month or so?"

So I did the rounds of the surgeries and was given a "no" after a "no" after a "no". I was now down to the very last doctor in the area, and happily he said, "Yes, I will look after your father". At this stage I have not met him and only spoke to him on the phone. As it happens in Australia, it seems that we import doctors from other countries, like we import goods from China – commodities as such. Most have names that are longer than my arm and I see consonants and vowels that are used in the most creative process. It was interesting when speaking to the receptionists of these surgeries – they did not attempt to pronounce the unpronounceable but would simply refer to the doctor as MJ or HY, etc. I do not have any issues with these doctors coming in, except I can't understand them, and often, I don't think they can understand me.

But who cares, Dad has a doctor, and more importantly for the nursing facility they had someone who would ultimately sign the death certificate. After all, the back must be protected with the right paperwork.

Me

Perhaps now is a good time to tell you bit about me and the work that I do. I write for a living, and have created a 'life style' business, whereby my office is where my notebook is. And so that is why throughout this missive, I often say that I sat at this place or at that table and worked. I have five or six books out, but alas, I have not made much money from them and so I have an author writing support service, which helps to pay the bills. But I must say, I am enjoying documenting this process, and who knows, perhaps this is the work that will immortalise me as a writer in the annals of history and make me wealthy beyond my dreams. Unlikely though, yet, to dream is good. But as I said, I am enjoying the process and find it cathartic. This is a difficult time for me, as it is the first time in my life I have been exposed to anything like this, whereby in the past I have scurried far away from this type of responsibility. When I say difficult, I am not sure if I am weak or inadequate in this way, but when I see 'that' man, who is my father, in that hospital bed slipping ever closer to madness and death it is hard to take. Then I go home to their place with Helen, it is like living in the psych ward, and so there is little or no respite. Other than Deborah, a lovely nurse, who has kindly adopted me in this town. I do not know anybody else here and so it is to my work and this writing that I turn to try and make sense of the process.

I do know that I am learning and that is always a good thing. For instance, I have learnt that I do not have to be right with Helen. It could be that I tell Helen something, and three or four minutes later she says to me, "Why did you not tell me that?" I could say, "But I did tell you". Or I could let it go and just explain it again. Knowing I do not have to be right all the time is probably a good thing for all of us and a lesson that will be good to hang on to for all life issues.

Another thing that I instinctively know is that I must ensure that my voice is always calm and positive and with no frustration in it. Because I can pretty much guarantee that the time that she will remember something will be the time that I was frustrated. She would remember the, "For God's sake Helen, can't you remember anything?"

It is imperative that that does not happen, otherwise all the trust flies out the window.

When I first started to document these happenings, it was more cathartic and for my own benefit. But then it occurred to me that perhaps others may derive benefit from this process and what I have learnt. Hopefully they will get a better understanding as to what Alzheimer's and other forms of dementia does to people and how it dismantles their life. I want people to know how difficult it is for the family members who become their support structure. It is important for people to appreciate that when someone has a form of dementia, that their memory structure is removed, therefore, so is their identity. Without an identity or ability to hold thoughts in their minds, they are locked in an empty time-zone. Because of the disease, they become inefficient at tasks that they found easy to do in the past and so get frustrated. Often, they are aware that they soil themselves, this not only embarrasses them, but it is uncomfortable. I could go on but throughout the book you should get the idea.

Another reason for writing it is to show you, that as good as our medical systems are, and the willingness of the medical staff, all is not perfect. Bureaucracy and inefficiencies kick in – often.

So if you are ever in this situation, you have to bully for results. This means you must take control and literally be the manager of your loved ones health.

Previously, there was a conversation with Helen, on one of our trips to Burnie, where she was anxious about Dad. She was also anxious about the path in front of her in terms of her dementia or Alzheimer's. She stated "Ten years ago there was absolutely no warning or indication as to what was to happen to me... and now... here I am in the grip of its horrific clutches. If only people knew what can confront them as a result of their partner dying, or worse, if they get the disease themselves. There is no preparation or way to handle this and although it is insipid in the way it creeps up on you, one minute you seem to be okay and the next you are like me, a quivering wreck".

16th July

Now that Dad is in the facility, although he is not cognitive enough to watch TV, we thought we would get him one, which may give him company. Helen said, "Please will you go and buy one and I will reimburse you later". But when I nosed around in the garage and found the stove, I also thought I saw a new TV, still in the box. So I went into the garage, and sure enough, there was a brand new set. Helen could not remember buying this. I wonder what other new and unused appliances could be lurking there.

Anyway, I took the TV up to Dad, but realised that an aerial had not been bought with the TV and so went and bought one. So now Dad has a noise box in his room, which he does not watch but the nurses turn it on on a daily basis.

Kim, my daughter, is a doctor and works in the public system in the emergency department. She has been a great help, especially this morning in a call that we had. And it is to do with what is known as an Advanced Directive. In some government institutions it is also called Goals of Care. They both seem to be the same thing, but it is confusing because someone who refers to goals of care may not know what an advanced directive is, and so if I mention an advanced directive they would not know what I was talking about. And of course the same applies and vice versa. I have also learnt that the advance directive is used in many parts of the world.

Essentially, it is a document that is signed by the loved ones, or the patient himself, providing the patient has the capacity to understand the process, whereby the treatment is aimed at extending the life of the patient unnaturally, or the not doing so.

Helen is most specific on this and does not want his life to be extended by unnatural means. In her forthright and clear way, she explains that when she grew up on the farm there were animals. When animals came to the end of their life they died. There was no point in trying to keep them here any longer, and that is the way of nature. For Lou (Dad) I do not want him to live any longer than his body wants. And when I go, she continued, I also do not want to be kept here any longer than what is natural.

I endorse what she says, but there is another reason for not unnaturally extending his life. And that his quality of life has diminished to the point where there is nothing meaningful going on in the brain. At close to ninety-three he is dying and it is only a matter of time. As there is no quality of life for him, he seems to have no capacity for happiness and joy, nor any intellectual ability or understanding. Then, that all being the case, there is no point in trying to extend that life unnaturally.

OH HELL
18th July

Today I was naughty. I felt the lounge was a bit higgledy-piggledy with too many disparate pieces of furniture that cluttered the room, making it look a bit like a second-hand furniture shop. I asked Helen, "How would you feel if we moved that couch against the wall so it is not in the way of the passage to the kitchen?"

Not deviating from past routines she said, "No I would rather leave it where it is thank you". But knowing she would not remember this I left it for half an hour and then asked her, "How do you feel if we moved the couch against the wall so that it is not in the way of the passage to the kitchen?"

"That's a very good idea", she said, "let's do it right now". And so we did and there it now lives against the wall.

One of my writing clients phoned me up and asked me how I was getting on. This client came into my life as a client about eighteen months ago but since then we have become good friends as well. I shall call him Author.

I remember clearly our first phone call; he had been given my details from someone who knew of my handholding service for new authors. He told me that he had written a few pieces and would I look at them for him. I could tell that he was nervous and thought that his work would not be of value, but he wanted to be sure. And so he emailed the piece through.

The writing was difficult to follow, with the longest sentences in the world and jam-packed with at least a dozen subjects in each. Paragraphs consumed pages and ideas were flung out like confetti at a wedding. When I received work like this from an author, I do not discount it because I know that with a bit of guidance the work can be improved, and so look at what is being said. Author's work is of a motivational theme with spiritual overtones so I looked at the relevance of what he was saying and whether it was unique, or was he just paraphrasing what many of the other motivational writer's write. The ideas were fresh, it was different, and he had the ability of teaching the same stuff (nothing is new) but in different way. Although it took me quite some time to wade through the difficulties of his writing, I enjoyed the directness and bravado in which he put his thoughts down.

I emailed him back and told him of my thoughts and that there is merit. I also edited the piece. The corrected document conveyed the same messages but it was forty percent shorter in length. Author phoned me back again, he disbelieved that I thought there was worth in his writing.

"Yes Author", I said, "you have a unique way of expressing your themes and I suggest that you continue. But we need to improve your writing skill over time. If you see the way that I edited your work you will get a sense of what I mean."

He went on to tell me that he had a full manuscript written and would I like to work through it for him? I agreed and then asked him has he done much writing?

He was a bit shy when he told me that this was not the only manuscript that he had as there was a second one, and even a third on the way. He then went on to say that he had many concepts that he wanted to write about and asked if he could send them to me as he finishes them?

"Yes, yes, by all means send them and let's try and clean the work up and see what we have later on."

He was enthusiastic and so the manuscript and a barrage of emails came with composed writings. Over the weeks and months I was able to confirm my original opinions of the value of his writing and on the concepts that he was getting across. He said that he liked the method that we were employing, whereby he would write a piece, I would edit it and send it back, and he would take in the edits.

Author, as I learnt, is highly intelligent, and so it did not take long for his writing to improve. So little by little, over a period of the about twelve months his writing was starting to be quite good. And as it did, so did his confidence, which came out in the way that he communicated his messages. Now the writing was strong and with purpose, and with this, his uniqueness was even more obvious.

From his various manuscripts and all the new writing, we have cobbled together three very good manuscripts. All are unique in what they teach and all reflect his personality and voice. I had been encouraging him to have this work published as I felt there would be many who would derive the benefit from his teachings. Because of his knowledge and ability, I suggested to him that he could be more than just an author and that he could hold workshops. I told him that with the writing and also with his presence as a speaker, then these would be a good combination. At first he discounted both but after a while he came around to believing that it was possible and that he would like to give it a go.

We were getting to the sharp end of his work where we were soon to publish and to build up his profile so as to get him known. And so early this morning he phoned me to see how things were going with Dad, but to also tentatively suggest that he fly down to me in Tasmania for the purpose of 'work-shopping' to further the process. He quickly went on to say that if I could spare the time, and that this might be a good distraction from the troubles that I had been facing. I couldn't agree more and was grateful for the suggestion of the interruption and the respite. I was also keen to further his progress.

So we rang off with him saying that he would try and fly in within the next two days. As Helen and Dad did not have too much on over the next few days I agreed and waited for him to arrive.

It is amazing how often we use the word remember in our speech. We say things like; "Remember that doctor's appointment last week: remember at breakfast we spoke about...", and so the word remember is ubiquitous and with few synonyms in our speech from which to use. And it came to my attention when tonight I said to Helen, "Remember that show we watched last week on the Trans-Siberian Railway trip?"

"No", she says, "I don't remember anything of the sort. Please don't use the words 'do you remember'". And of course I get caught out every couple of days where I say remember this or remember that and each time I get the same reply.

"Hi Deborah", I said as I answered her phone call, "how are you?" "Good cupcake". Lots of people are her cupcake."Wanna go out for a drink tonight?" She asked.

"Is the Pope a Catholic?" I answered. "Why, what's the deal?"

"We're celebrating our graduation and meeting down at the local pub at six."

After what I had been going through over the last week I needed no excuse for a beer and so said, "Yep, see you at six".

Needless to say, I got there at six-fifteen, not wanting to be early, and everyone else got there at about 7:30. Thank God for smart phones and Internet of which I used to pass the time. But as Deborah took me to the table there were about twelve of her nursing buddies. Over the time I chatted to this one and chatted to that one and forgot the problems that enveloped my life.

24th of July

Today was the first 'check-in' appointment for the ACAT contract support program that I have put in place for Helen. Helen must've asked me about six times beforehand, "What is this appointment for?" And with each explaining she was quite comfortable with it. Anyway the lady came and was able to ease Helen's mind.

Wanting them to be able to do this without my involvement, I went into the dining room, ostensibly to work. I made sure the work that I did was not mind consuming so I could monitor the conversation as I needed to know its direction. But it was good and easy and I think the consultant had a good grasp of the situation. I did have a quick chat with her before she left so that she was aware that if she saw any decline in Helen then she would record and monitor it. As I mentioned earlier I wanted Helen to retain as much independence as possible, especially for when I headed off again.

Only a quick visit with Dad today and whilst there, two carers came in to take him into the toilet. Once inside, they close the door, to give me and him a bit of privacy. But I could hear through the door the young nurse say, "No Lou, don't spit at us".

I then heard him say, "I will get a gun and shoot you".

I thought it time to end the visit for the day.

I learnt something about Helen today. When she was getting to know the contract care worker, the lady asked Helen if she had children.

"No", was the reply. "My mother had Huntington's disease. Huntington's disease usually causes movement disruptions, cognitive and psychiatric disorders with a wide spectrum of signs and symptoms. I did not want to pass that gene down to my child".

I knew of her mother having Huntington's and Helen's concern. I did not know that this was the reason for her conscious decision to not have kids. When I was here for her attempted suicide, I had her tested for Huntington's. This took some doing as she really thought that her symptoms were those of Huntington's, and so was scared to have it confirmed. But fortunately I convinced her and she went. Happily, the results were negative.

Author flew in this afternoon, and hired a car from the airport and drove to his hotel in the centre of Devonport. We are to start workshoping tomorrow morning.

25th of July

We had been working in author's hotel room for about four hours, when he suggested that we adjourn to the pub for a beer and lunch. And so we did. Whilst there we chatted about many subjects and finally moved on to the situation with Dad and Helen.

"This is a very noble thing that you are doing", said Author.

"Noble, not from my point of view it is. For me to suggest that what I'm doing is noble would also have to suggest that there is some sort of grand sacrifice or hardship that I'm undergoing and aware of undergoing in this process. I rather see it as something that I have to do, and something that I will do, irrespective of any difficulties that there are."

"Good point", said author, "but nevertheless it is noble…"

Back in the motel room we were working and talking and I started to get a bad feeling. I know the feeling, it is one where I know I'm going to have to do something which is likely to hurt and upset. For some time I've noticed Author's becoming more and more superior. This is incongruous with his teachings and what he is to offer. The attitude suggests that all must listen to him irrespective – as he's always correct. I'm thinking that he has so much brilliance and can really help many people but this aspect of his character is not in sync with the work that he wants to do. If he was selling real estate or luggage and he had that attitude it wouldn't matter as much. But as he is teaching self-worth and spiritual values, to show his audience a better way, to me it needs humility and integrity. As this trip of his was only our second physical meeting I was getting to know him better, and was starting to have misgivings.

We reach about 5 o'clock and the red wine comes out, a local brand from the cellar door just down the road. It's okay but nothing startling. And in our chatting he intimated, "what if I became his business manager in this affair". Although this was said as if it was a sudden spur of the moment thought, all Author's suggestions are considered and weighed well in advance.

Because of my ill feeling, I wanted to buy time, for I did not think that this was the right time to bring up my misgivings. But I also wanted him to know that I may choose otherwise. So I said to him, "Why me, by accepting I'm moving from my core competencies and you'd probably do better with someone who knows what they are doing".

"Yes", he said, "you could be but you are still likely to do a better job".

I then said, "I'm not sure, but let me think about". Thinking about this now, I know that I am not going to accept.

26th of July

I said to Author that we were near the end of our discussions and so why don't we take a drive around the area and chat as we go. So this morning he picked me up at 10 o'clock and we headed inland to do a circuit that would take about four hours, plus lunch. It was a lovely drive, everything was green and lush, the road upped and downed, and many curves, across full-flooded rivers and past snow-capped mountains, seeing interesting homesteads cockily ensconced on hilltops and by creeks, the cows, horses and sheep with crows flying, the grey sky that every so often opened up to blue, only to return back to grey, light rain becoming sleet and becoming rain again, interesting little towns, some that had murals plastered over the various buildings. Other villages had unique post boxes outside the houses, such as a tractor turned into a post box, or one with a fairy, another an old motorbike.

And we chatted, sometimes about work, and sometimes about what we saw. We pulled into Sheffield where Author had a coffee and I had a green tea. We both had a pie and continue chatting. It is a very nice way of conducting business and we had pretty much finalised all that we had to discuss.

And as we were heading back I said to Author, "What about a beer?"

"Absolutely", he said. "I have seen a pub opposite the Mersey River and thought that it might be nice to sit in there where we should be able to see the river." Half an hour later we were firmly ensconced at a table against the window, which had a perfect view of the river. And so we chatted some more. We needed to design the book cover, but one that is likely to also become a kind of logo. It would carry a theme that would go through all Author's books. So it was a brainstorm session. We generated some good ideas.

I noticed a ship that was on the other side of the river spurt smoke that wasn't spurting before. So I said, "Seems like they have turned on the boilers, perhaps they are about to head out".

About fifteen minutes later we could see that there was movement with the boat. But here is the thing, the ship was facing inland, the same way as it would have done as it steamed up the river to its docking and so we wondered how it would get out and postulated; perhaps there will be a tug that somehow pushes it around. It will be difficult to do as the length of the ship is probably not much shorter than the width of the river. Perhaps tugs would tow it backwards? Or maybe it would steam up river a bit further to a wider section of the river. And as we sat and watched we saw that the bow of the ship started sliding towards us whilst the stern remained static. We wondered if there is was tug on the other side that we can't see pushing the bow outwards. Irrespective, this is going to be an interesting exercise because clearly the boat was turning at right angles to the river, especially with the ship being almost as long as the river is wide. It took about fifteen minutes for the ship to be at right angles to the river with not much distance between the stern or bow and land. There was no tug involved and the ship was turning under its own power and control. Marvellous we wondered, what a feat of pilot-ship. And then we got onto the theory or probability that this maneuver could only be done at an ebb tide because it would be difficult to do if it was done with a tide running briskly in or out. We googled tides for Devonport and it showed that yes, it is about the ebb tide. But how do they do it when windy, and Devonport gets really windy? There was another ship on the river, that was next to the cement works but

OH HELL

this ship had already been turned around was facing towards the mouth of the river. And so more deep drinks of beer and questions came where we suggested that the cement carrying ship is turned before it is loaded, because if it is loaded and turned, perhaps the weight would be too great and it might run aground. Once the ship had gone we turned our attention back to the book cover image.

It was about the fifth beer that we wandered onto a different topic, or rather Author did, and this was about the situation with Helen.

"I think you're wasting your time with this situation." My jaw must have dropped as I waited for him to continue, which he did.

"You see what you are doing for Helen is not helping her in the long run. In fact it is detrimental to her and the reason being is that it will be far better that you get her into a care facility now, rather than later. After all, there would be twenty-four hour help and support, there would be social engagement with other residents and the like."

I agreed that he may be right and that I had looked at this and even made the suggestion. But sometimes what seems right is not right in the specific instance, such as this one.

"You didn't hear me", he interrupted me, "what I'm saying is right and you're not listening". As he said this is voice became louder and aggressive with the suggestion that 'why don't you take what I'm saying is right and do what I say is right'.

I waited for him to stop and finally he did. I related a conversation that I had with Helen about two weeks earlier where I suggested we look seriously at that possibility of her going into a home now, after all, she may like the idea. Helen's short-term memory may be bad but her logic and reasoning is spot on, and I respect it and listen to it. We spoke about all the pros and cons of it happening and at the end she turned round and said, "I do not know how much time I have left and I really want to have as much quality time as possible. If I go into the facility I will not be able to keep my dog. Nor am I near this beautiful beach and coastline and it means that I wouldn't have enjoyable walks with my dog. I will not have my garden to work in, and as you know the garden gives me focus".

Author persisted and said, "It wouldn't take long for this facility to be like home".

Again, I disagreed by saying, "She has a home and the facility would not be anywhere near as good as her home. You know, I do expect her to muddle through many things when I'm not here but most of them will not be life or death issues and so some of them will be mere annoyances, perhaps like forgetting to put the garbage out for three weeks in a row, or not paying a fine, which then incurs interest. So what if a creditor doesn't get paid, or the milk does not get bought. How could I, someone who lives with so much independence in life, and always have, try to curtail her short time left by reducing her independence? You know Author, if we only gain her three months then it will be worth it. But hopefully we gain her several years. Make no mistake she's clever and she knows her inadequacies and she will know when the inadequacies become too much for her and I'm sure that I will receive a phone call saying, please come and help me and get me into the facility. And when that happens I will do so".

But, also being who he is, he tried again. "You are being foolish, don't you realise that you're sacrificing your business? You should be working fourteen hours a day to create the thrust to give it traction?..." He went on and on and on. In the end I interrupted him and said to him, "Author you are smart and you're wise, and you can really help people. But there is an incongruous aspect to your nature and that is that you have to be right all the time, irrespective of the circumstances. You have to be right, therefore everyone else must be wrong. In fact, you have to be so right that you will verbally bludgeon your opponent until such time they become submissive. Author, in this instance you are wrong".

He spluttered about three times saying, "You... you.... you fool, you just don't listen". Then he stopped for a while, and seethed – the atmosphere explosive.

Finally he asked, "And so where does that leave us and our relationship?"

I am impetuous at the best of times, but when I have beers in me I'm even more so, and of course coupled with the misgivings that I related earlier, I simply said, "It's time to go our separate ways. I think the work that you are doing is fantastic and I really wish you well".

Softening my tone a bit I continued, "I intimated yesterday that we would probably think better about going our own way as I have helped you as much as perhaps I can, and certainly as much as I want to. So I shall finish up what I'm working on and then raise a final invoice to you".

Jumping off his bar stool, "You are an idiot", he said, "here you are with your fledgling business and you are dumping your biggest client. How dumb is that?"

"It's not dumb at all, you see I do not live in fear and believe that I can attract into my life the abundance that I deserve. Whether that is with you and your work or not. It will still happen for me. I have enough belief in myself and my ability and know that what I'm doing, by passing you up as client will merely be a blip in the big scheme of things, and that down the line, in a years' time it would not have had any major effect".

With all that beer inside me I needed to go and release some of it so got up and said, "I'll be back in a minute".

When I returned, Author had tears in his eyes and was full of remorse, and as I sat down he put out his hand and put it on mine. He is not gay and nor am I, and so I could see that he was really trying to reach out to me with all his heart. He apologised and said, he had been a fool and could I forgive him.

"Sure, of course I do… but I still think it is better that I let you go."

He then said that he recognises that what I said about him, having to be right, and that he will try to modify his behaviour.

I in turn said, "Author you have so much to offer mankind in your writing and your teaching, with all your wisdom and insight, but even so, I recognise that you can never ever be 100% perfect all the time, nor do I expect you to be perfect. But in this instance all that is really required is that you do acknowledge aspect of your character and mitigate it as best as you can. We all have issues, some are allowed to run wild, which isn't the wise thing to do.

But Author, there is more I need to say to you. I can't work with you for another reason and that is that I don't believe that... that... you are always living the precepts of what you are wanting to teach..."

As we said good night, He said he would phone in the morning before he flew out, I'm wondering if he will.

27th July

Today I woke up with a hangover, but still feel better than I have after spending days with Dad and Helen. I reflect on the argument and feel that what I did was right.

I normally wake up fairly early and start working, but stop and have breakfast with Helen as a way to touch base with her and to see how she is. As we sit down, the first question that she asks is, "What is this appointment on the calendar for today?"

Of course I tell her again, as I did last night, and as I will probably have to do three or four more times before the appointment happens. But that's OK as I am prepared for the question, which came to me twice during the meal.

Breakfast time is usually an easy time for us, as once being an inherently organised person, the preparation routine is well entrenched, and so she prepares on auto. Often, she will want to know every single detail. This can be frustrating as sometimes I'm explaining things for forty minutes at a time – it's frustrating mainly because she usually forgets what I say and asks again. In many respects it would be so much easier if she just let me get on with it and direct accordingly, which is what always happens anyway. It does waste a lot of time, but I understand her need for (imagined) control.

At lunchtime, she says, "I think I will go into town and browse for a while".

"Okay" I replied "but said please be back at 2:45 so as we can go to the appointment."

What appointment?

Oh Gawd, I think, when this is all over, my caravan and another life calls me. Please let this not go on for too long.

"The appointment at the care facility for Dad. People are coming to assess him and they need to ask us questions."

Of course, she went out and forgot the appointment, I had to re-schedule for an hour later.

It's 2 o'clock in the morning and I'm writing. Normally, in the evening I'm too tired to write, and usually crash about 10 o'clock. But often I wake up about 2 o'clock, refreshed and so turn my attention to writing for an hour before falling asleep again for the last session of the night before waking up in the morning.

As I write I wonder, was today, or rather yesterday, a bad day or a good day. Did I have compassion and was I gentle and supportive of Helen and Dad?

I quickly glance at the current load of admin paperwork to see if I had done all that there was to do for both Helen and Dad. It is good that I dropped off the form at the funeral parlour, so other than a few questions that they are likely to ask that is pretty much taken in hand. One thing less to worry about. Oh yes, must write the words for the plaque.

We had the appointment, and it transpired to be a governmental practitioner from Hobart who came to assess him. Apparently this had been done twice before but I was not aware of these. But it was good that we were there because I learned some interesting things. For instance; the medication that they put Dad on, to improve his temperament was causing other effects, such as the stiffening of his arm muscles. So he will reduced the quantity and will monitor from there.

He seem to think that dad was looking a little bit better, which is a good thing. His main reason for being there is not so much to prolong life, but to make Dad's life more comfortable for the time left. I then spoke to him about the Advanced Directive. He said, that even with the form that I had filled out that it is a bit pointless if I don't get the GP to agree to it. As explained earlier, Dad's GP was newly appointed and so I need to make an appointment with him tomorrow.

The practitioner was a male and of Belgium heritage and spoke with a strong accent. He felt that Dad had plateaued and that his decline wasn't quite as fast as what it seemed to be before. So I asked him the inevitable question, "Is there any way of understanding where he is in the process?

In his strong accent he said, "Vell it von't be the dementia that kills him, it vill be a complication". I nodded my head in understanding and he continued, "The options are..." Not a great turn of phrase to use under the circumstances but there was no malice in it and his selection was an unfortunate choice of English. I let him continue uninterrupted and he said, "There vas no vay of knowing if and vhen any complications may come. And then of course there is still the heart issue, vhich might give out at any moment. But it is possible that you still have your father in several months".

What he also explained was that there is a thing called a Guardianship Authority, which basically gives one the right to make suggestions for treatment, and this is most important with the Advanced Directive. I learnt that the Power of Attorney, which Helen has for Dad, is for financial reasons only, and that is why the guardianship is required for medical support. But here is the thing, to gain a Guardianship one must apply to the Guardianship board (yes another board), which could take several months.

Now back to the impending appointment with the GP, I am hoping that he is not all that familiar with those rules and just assumes that I do have the right.

I have been considering what I have learnt about the care and the role of the Advanced Directive. As stated, Helen and I do not want to unnaturally prolong Dad's life. What is administered must be with the intention of making him comfortable and without pain. But herein lies the dilemma, what about infection? Suppose he got an infection of the throat, this is unlikely to have an effect on his demise, or could it? And so we would want this to be treated because we would not want him to be in any discomfort. Taking into consideration what we heard, "That it is not the dementia that will kill him, he is likely to die of complications". So what if the bad throat got worse, and developed into pneumonia? Pneumonia is a definite complication that could bring on Dad's death, so in effect, the treating of a sore throat could in fact be contravening the Advanced Directive. What about an infection in the kidney? By treating this, they could be unnaturally extending his life. Nothing is straight forward.

A carer, or nurse is trained to help heal. To improve the comfort of the patient, and so their natural instinct is to give treatment for the sore throat or kidney infection.

I can see that this process is full of landmines, and sort of let them get away with these comfort making procedures.

28th July

Upon walking in to Dad's room today, he looked thoughtfully at me and said, "I'm glad you are here 'John' (my brother John)". He then mumbled, "When you (John) have your drink on Sunday, you must bring me some back as I'm bloody bored in here".

This is probably the most lucid thing he has said in the six weeks that I've been here. Except I don't know where he thought I, or John, go on Sunday to 'pot it up'.

Today I do some of the admin pertaining to the care facility. The first batch of invoices arrived, which of course was higher than what we were lead to believe it would be – but of course, it is always that way. But it was not the facilities fault, it was more to do with the government's 'means test' calculation, and so the monthly bill was around $5,000. Fortunately they can afford it, and he needs the care.

At dinner it took about three quarters of an hour to re-explain to Helen the funding until she understood, again. And what she heard in the appointment with the aged care doctors, she was satisfied with the result but tired at the end of the day.

29th of July

The appointment with the doctor went well as he was of the same mindset as we were – that to prolong Dad's life would be to prolong misery. And so he signed the form that I gave him. Hooray!

This doctor, as I explained above, was virtually the last one in the district who we approached to look after The Old Man, and although I would not like to use the term the last resource, in fact he was. This chap comes from Africa and is dark, very dark. He is also large, very large. And he told me that he went to visit and introduce himself to Dad but as Dad was in one of his more delirious states where he was a bit aggressive, the doctor, who I shall call The Doctor for sensitivity sake, decided not to see Dad on that occasion and quietly backed out of the room. The reason being, is that he felt that if Dad saw this very large and very dark apparition materialise in front of him then Dad might freak! How astute is that? Because that is exactly what I think Dad would have done. The doctor and I had a good chuckle about this. Nice man and I have confidence in him as my father's doctor.

However, I do want the doctor to examine Dad and so I suggested that when he knows he's going to go to the facility that I make sure Helen is on hand to pacify Dad. The doctor thought this a good idea

OH HELL

and he is likely to phone me, probably about the weekend, for this to happen.

In all previous visits Dad has not been coherent enough to really talk about death or even that he is in a nursing care facility for old people who are waiting for the inevitable. In fact, in many instances he has not even acknowledged being there. But today was different, as today there was an indication that he knew where he was and in a few seconds of soundbite he asked, "Is everyone here going to die?" The implication of this was that he had been brought to this place of death and that he would soon be heading down that corridor.

For a man who fears death this is a scary scenario, however it is a step in the right direction of acceptance. As a writer, I am a man of many words but when he asked me that question none that were of any value would come. Fortunately, when Dad asked the question there was a nurse in the room and her quick response was. "No Dearie, they have just come here to rest and to be looked after in comfort".

I was watching Dad's face when she said it and I could see him thinking about this, and after a time, there was a slight nod of his head as if he accepted that explanation, seemed satisfied that he was not soon to be pushed down that corridor.

I was pleased to see that at last he recognised that he was in a place for the old, and that there is acceptance.

My father has always been afraid of death. Over the years as he got older, occasionally I or someone else broached the subject. Upon doing so he would become agitated and with firmness change the subject – he simply would not tolerate the thought of it. This is sad in a way as death could be a time of crowning glory and also fulfilment. It can be a time of acceptance.

I would think that it would be easier to accept death than to be in fear of it as it moves to claim us, whereby the mind can compose itself for what is happening. It would be more about accepting with grace, and not fighting it with fear. For my part I do not fear death, well not the actual dying part. Perhaps the leading up to it could be pretty crappy as who wants to lose health, independence and mental ability?

I read recently that we never just die. We die when we give up or let go. It could be that when he had that heart attack and that his body was not really strong enough to live, but he lived anyway, and keeps living because he does not accept death and therefore does not give up. If this is the case then I would expect, that little by little, the resistance will diminish as he will be too tired to fight it.

Maybe acceptance for him requires time, and that is why he is hanging on as he is doing, and excuse the pun of which I can't resist, of hanging on for dear life. But I feel once he has come to accept it, even if only in his sub conscious, then the process will gain momentum, and once it does, perhaps a bit like a slippery dip, once he is sliding down it there is no stopping the process.

Elizabeth Kubler Ross dedicated her life to working with the dying so as she, and the elderly, can understand the process and to give a language from which to discuss death and to open a narrative on the facing of death. She documented her work in various books, of which *On Death and Dying* is the most prominent.

A psychiatrist, Kubler Ross was the recipient of twenty honorary degrees and by July 1982 had taught, in her estimation, 125,000 students in death and dying courses in colleges, seminaries, medical schools, hospitals, and social-work institutions.

Within her work she explains that when people comes to grips with the impending death, then there is greater peace within, and often, as an interesting side effect, that this usually supports and helps the people who are at the bedside of the person dying. So I wonder that if Dad did except his death then it might be easier for Helen.

My thought of the need to accept death, in some part of our conscious mind, before death happens, certainly is not correct for people who are in some sort of impact accident, such as being hit by a bus and dying instantly. But it does seem a logical acceptance process when death, perhaps dying of cancer, or age when the time has come.

OH HELL

And then there is Helen who grew up on a farm and saw death to animals on a regular basis. When it was their time, they went and that's all there was to it. And so the same is with us humans – when it is our time it will be our time and that's all there is to it. In conversations with her about death, and specifically about her ultimate death, she is afraid of it. When I asked her why she is afraid, she said because it is not what she is familiar with, which I take to mean that she is afraid of the process of dying but not the after death. Because, in her own words, "That our soul does not soar in the ether for evermore, therefore, there is nothing".

She is agnostic and does not believe in religion of any sort. And although she went to a Christian school as a child, she scoffs at religious bodies. Yet, she would not try and stop anybody from pursuing or enjoying their religion, because if that is what they want to do and want to believe in, then good for them. But she does not believe in any sort of continuance after physical death.

Yet most of modern humanity are afraid of death – why? Most do not leave adequate instructions for their loved one's as to what they want pertaining to their death. The topic is skirted around by both the dying and their living family, where all are weary to say or think too much about it.

And I guess it would be wrong to record all these thoughts without giving mine. I live with spiritual beliefs, whereby I am in gratitude for all that there is. I have reverence for life, the planet and this incredible opportunity to be here and to be all that we can be. I am not religious, and the rituals of most religions, to my mind do not get me closer to our creator, but I am happy for you to be so and I would never try to convince you that your religion is wrong. Religion can be a great comfort in times of need, or even just as support in life.

Some of my beliefs come from Buddhism, which to me is about acceptance and simplicity. Love, that is universal love, also plays a big part in my life. I'm also influenced by the teachings from the indigenous races of the world such as, the Australian Aborigine or the natives of America. The teachings of being at one with all fits very well within my logic. It is through their teaching that I have such love and acceptance for Mother Nature and all existence.

But back to Dad; it is hard to understand his non-acceptance of death as I explained above, when one considers that he had the most hideous time in the Second World War, that he would have been exposed in the most graphic detail to the deaths of literally thousands of people and that death is a normal aspect of life. Many of those would have been his comrades in arms. And many would have been the so-called opposition, and many are likely to have been innocent civilians who happened to get caught up in man's folly.

Speaking to Enid (The Mum who stepped in to raise John and I. Will explain later) on the phone earlier, we were talking about Dad and his war years. She related a story where once she wore green eyeshadow. The Old Man freaked and told her to take it off straight away as her eyes looked like the eyes of dead Russians. So clearly, he has seen much death.

I do not wish to suggest that seeing death on such a grand scale cheapens life, on the contrary, it could give greater meaning to life. But surely, when one sees death as he would have done, then there would have been acceptance that death does happen and that his own mortality is just a wink in the grand scheme of time? If Dad could accept his finite time here and realise that if life continued forever, there is no doubt that at some stage we would want to end it with a death. Life is beautiful because it is finite. It is this finite capacity that gives it its value.

Clearly from our very earliest thoughts we know about death and its inevitability, yet for many, including my dad, this knowledge is suppressed. And usually the reason why it is suppressed is because of the fear of death. Death is an unknown, death in many respects is out of our control and we love to be in control. Death is about our ego, and how everybody can survive without us once we have gone. Our survival instinct is natural and is subtly influencing virtually every thought and action that we take. But yet, our death instinct should also be natural and although not necessarily a constant part of our awareness, it should be there to support us, not only when we're going, the when our loved ones go as well.

Now I'm not just talking about Dad's acceptance of death, I'm talking about how comforting it would be to any dying person, and all the loved ones, if death was openly discussed. I would think in the process all love would be shared among the family if they were able to openly discuss it. But because it's not referred to, then it is less likely that the love will be allowed to enter that space. How sad is that? Yes, when someone is dying you can show your love but if you were constantly sidestepping the issue because the person dying or anyone else does not accept that fact, then the full quota of love that needs to be expressed before the person passes over is never likely to happen.

For instance, I believe that Helen is already grieving the death of her husband, even before he passes over. He has gone from the house, never to return, and to Helen, that is already his death. Additionally, the fact that he is not conscious to her, is also another sign of his death – he is already lost to her. I'm sure that if he was more cognitive and able to express and accept that he was dying, then she would be more able to express that love and grief to him. But because she can't, it stays sealed within her.

I would suggest the part of the problem is one of western society, which has an aversion to death because of that fear and the unknown, and so that it is not an open discussion. Whereas, the indigenous peoples of the world have a far healthier and more natural way of understanding death and living with its potential.

Often I wonder if I should broach the subject with him. Today, when sitting there I thought about saying, "Dad, do you know you are dying?" But it does not feel right to say that as I don't think I am close enough to him. But what would happen if I did? He might freak. I think if anyone was to open the subject up of his death, it should be Helen. Dad trusts her implicitly and is likely to accept what she says and by doing so it would pave the way for that openness. But once again, even as positive as this is likely to be, I don't think I have the right to say this to Helen as this is likely to put additional stress on her and at this stage that is unlikely to be good for her. Who knows though, it may be cathartic for her in her grief. I have more to ponder on this, and will keep my mind open in case an opportunity presents itself where I can easily suggest this.

31st July

Today we drove through to Burnie for Helen's MRI scan. Helen was calm about it as she kept forgetting what we going to do there and what reason, so she enjoyed the outing. "I don't know if I told you but about 20 years ago…"

But before heading out of town we popped in to see Dad for half an hour and taking him a photo of Helen and Zoe. I took the photo this morning on my phone and then had it developed and bought a frame. We put it on his bedside table and when he saw us do this he looked at the photo, then at Helen and realised who the photo was of. There was, or there seem to be, a slight smile on his face. And I am not sure if I should be happy or annoyed. I have been here now for six weeks and in that time Dad has not recognised me as being Pat – not once. There have been a couple of times when he recognised me as one of his sons but a 'no name-brand' son. If I am allocated a name, it is that of John. But as soon as Dad saw the photo, he said, "There she is… … there is Zoe. How is she?" So Zoe the dog, obviously has a higher rating than Pat the son!

After the MRI, Helen said, "That was quick, I was expecting it to be hours". In my teasing voice (I have been told I use a teasing voice when I tease) I replied, "That is probably because there is not much brain in there to work on!" She laughed about as much as I did. I tend to like my own jokes.

Leaving the MRI appointment, it was a late afternoon appointment and the whole process took about two hours. As we headed along the coastal highway in Friday afternoon traffic, it seemed more frantic than normal. Clearly people are in a hurry to get home and start the weekend, or perhaps they have started and are rushing to a weekend destination. Either way, both Helen and I are pensive – I am driving, and happy to let everybody rush past me. Tonight's glass of red wine will go down very nicely indeed.

OH HELL

Whilst talking about teasing; a few weeks ago Helen cooked dinner. When she starts to do so I say nothing and let her get on with it. But most times I cook, But occasionally she may say, "I'll cook dinner tonight".

But yet, nothing happens, she forgets.

But about this tease. A few weeks ago she just started to cook, so I let her go, but thought it was earlyish, like an hour early. She, being of the farming community got into the habit of eating at six PM, as according to that fraternity, this is a sensible time to eat. So when dinner arrived at 4:45 PM I said nothing and climbed in (even though I was kind of full after eating carrot cake with Deborah only any hour earlier). But when she went to turn on the news, which is what one does in this house after dinner, there was no such news. Scrutinising the clock, she realised she was well over an hour early. We laughed, and then I said that there is no fun teasing an Alzheimic person about cooking earlier, because the next day she would not remember the cooking or the teasing.

Of course we have not been given the results of the scan as they will be given to the Geriatrician who in turn will give them to us. So more waiting.

1st August

Not a good day today. Helen started to pack some of Dad's clothes away. Away, into a box, but not as far as the shed, or even the charity. Packing each item, which she had ironed a thousand times, and seen him wear them just as many times, was just too much for her. So now, the sorrowful items reside in the box, on her bedroom floor, where each time she sees them it bring waves of pain. The handkerchief was severely strangled today.

A friend of mine sent me an email to see how I am getting on. This is my reply.

> Hi Jenny
>
> It's so nice to have so many friends who are supporting me in this process. Thank you very much for your thoughts.
>
> Dad is now out of the hospital and into an aged care facility, which is much better in terms of the treatment, and also closer so we don't have to spend hours in the car.
>
> He has deteriorated a lot, but still could hang around for several months. The timeframe is his and his alone.
>
> Helen, has big swings of ups and downs. The downs are shit!
>
> At first this entire process was stressing me, but I seem to have settled into it and with the long walks along the beautiful headlands, meditation and the odd glass of wine I think I am coping well.
>
> Much love Pat

Helen has always been on top of her banking and personal accounts, upfront in paying her bills and never having creditor problems. Probably about eight years ago she bought a computer to help facilitate the payment of accounts and things, which worked well, until such time as her brain started to slow down. And I know on all my various visits here I was always resetting up equipment and getting things going again for her, only to learn that the next time there I needed to do it again.

She also enjoyed Internet browsing and she would learn all sorts of things with great interest. And so on this trip, as yet again nothing is working. As she likes browsing I thought it may be a good idea for her to get an iPad. These are definitely easier to use than a normal PC is. I also felt that it would be good for her to use this device to help stimulate her and her brain. I also plan to download and install brain exercises that she could use that might help her.

After discussing it with her, she liked the idea and so we went and acquired one.

OH HELL

Alas, it was not so easy to teach her, as even with the making of the simplest notes, she has difficulties, such as what I said earlier about the new telephone instructions. For about ten days in a row we 'played' with the iPad, and she just could not get it. What she saw yesterday was like it never happened. This is most unfortunate because it could have been really good for her, whilst helping her. But all that it succeeds in doing is to frustrate her. When we were at Shrink's next appointment, she made the suggestion of forgetting about the iPad because the frustration could aggravate her condition. But Helen being who she is, always wanting to learn and use her brain, and also forgetting Shrink's advice, would grab the device every so often and give it a go. Invariably she forgets that we had made notes (I bought her a notepad for that specific purpose and made the suggestion that she nicely cover it, much the same as children do with schoolbooks), and so I would take the book off the table and show it to her and remind her that she had made notes. "Oh", she would say almost every time, "I wondered what this was for". She will start working through the notes with me in support but most of the time I would end up doing the full search for her. Next day, I might say something like, "How was that article on the Everglades that you read last night?" She would look at me and say "what article?"

The psychologist also suggested that I buy an appointment book for Helen and that all her various appointments and requirements be put in it under the relevant date and time. We all agreed that this would be a good thing to do. So the diary was bought and used once, and forgotten about. Every so often I would take it out and repopulate the necessary appointments and tasks but each time she came across it she wonder's what it was for.

2nd August

What is really important for Helen is that she feels that she is able to contribute. Ever since I have known her she has always been involved in some sort of charitable work. For instance, for many years she was involved in doing work for various guide dog associations, or seeing-eye dogs as they are often referred to. Her efforts are consistent but humble. Most people do not know of the work that she has done over the years. And even now she knits little squares about 100 mm × 100 mm that are sown together to make blankets for dogs and cats at the RSPCA. These blankets are put under the animal so they do not have to lie on the cold concrete. To save money, she goes to charities like the St Vincent De Paul Society and buys old woolen pullovers. Then in her lounge chair she spends hours unravelling them, making them into big balls, some of which I am sure are several kilometres long. Then she starts the process of converting the balls into the little squares, prior sewing together. Goodness knows how many she has made over the years.

Making these blankets is a bit mindless, but she likes this as it keeps her active but is restful on the mind. But she feels that she wants to contribute more, especially now with this process. She needs to be socialised (seems that this term us used mainly for puppies) and so we have talked about her doing an hour a week at a charity, sorting or washing clothes, cleaning or anything. Does not matter what she does as long as she helps, and in the process of helping she meets people. There has to be more in her life than her dog, her dying husband, and me, when I am around, which hopefully will not be forever.

We have spoken about this often, but we both felt that with the driving to Burnie as we were doing and the stress of Dad's condition that we wait. But the other day, she was remorseful and suicidal in as much as she bemoaned that her use as a person is over. That there was not much point to life and that once Dad goes, she must go as well. This is a regular thought that she has, and quite frankly, I don't know how to counteract it. Yes, I try and get her to see the value of life, that her walks with Zoe, along these magnificent beachfronts and headlands; her garden and any other interest. One of these would be to help at a charity and offer her value.

OH HELL

3rd August

Tough visiting today. Helen stayed at home as she needed respite from it all, so I went and as soon as I saw him I knew he was agitated. He was trying to get out of bed, to go home. But he does not have the strength to stand up and the few times he tried to get out of bed he fell over and remained on the floor until someone came. When he saw me he shouted, "Bloody bitches", and then, referring to the small carry bag I had with me, "What shit are you bringing?"

After a time he said "I need to pee", and so I called the carer. When she came and I relayed the message. She said that she would call another, as they need two. But in the end they needed four to help, such was his agitation. He was like this the entire time I stayed – most uncomfortable.

That poor man, who for most of his adult life has been imprisoned by a mind stocked with memories of horror. Now, he's captive of the mind that is governed by a shrunken brain and damaged brain cells.

But I had to laugh when I got home. On the way I did some shopping and bought some grapes as Helen likes them. She had stopped buying them about two weeks ago as the price went up considerably. Obviously the previous in-season made way to stored older grapes. When she saw the grapes, I said, "I know you like them so bugger the price". She moaned, but ate some anyway.

After a time I said, "Funny what you remember and what you don't. You will forget an appointment or whether or not you have fed Zoe... and you left Zoe out the other night, but you remember that you do not buy grapes because the price has gone up".

"Damn right", she shot back, "last week (about three weeks ago really) they were $7.55 a kg, but now they are $14.00 a kg, so no, I won't buy them!"

It was difficult growing up in Dad's household as a child, for we could not comprehend what drove him. And there were many instances, here is another:

I think that it was Keith, my elder brother, who brought the kitten home. I must have been about ten at the time. It was tiny, only about four-weeks old and was jet black. John, Keith and I instantly loved it and kept it hidden from Dad, who didn't like cats.

For two weeks we kept it hidden but Dad eventually discovered it. After the lecture on the evils of cats, he grabbed it and told us, "Come." He drove us to the local rubbish dump, some five or six kilometres away and ditched it. Then rubbing his hands together in a manner of – now that was easy enough, said, "No more cat". We were devastated as we drove away, leaving a forlorn Kitty on top of a pile of junk.

The story does not end here, as about ten days later, Kitty, like a homing pigeon, somehow found his way back. This was truly miraculous and defies logic, yet there he was. We did not even have time to fatten him up, when again he was discovered by Dad. Rolling his sleeves up he said, "I vill now do the job properly." He got a bag out of the shed and put a brick and kitty into it and tied the top. We were told, "Stay here," as he and the bag drove towards the beach. Upon his return he told us with glee that he had thrown the bag into the ocean.

Poor Kitty, even he could not Houdini his way out of that one. We were heart broken and it took a long time before we would speak to him again. And certainly we would not bring any more cats home, as we were too petrified he would find out.

For many years I hated my father, but I have softened my approach as a result of doing much 'head-work' on myself. And for the last twenty years I have tried to understand what he went through and what made him like that. There were many more incidents but there is no need to highlight these, nor is there a need to keep them alive. Do I love my father? I can't honestly say that I do. But yet, I'm here for him and Helen — we humans are strange folk.

OH HELL

Throughout this work I have written what I need to write for my own self-preservation. The astute among you will recognise the low days, and also the high days. For authenticity sake, and also for the cathartic aspect, I do not try to mask my emotion – it is what it is.

Most of my days are taken up with; either visiting Dad, the management of his care, and supporting Helen with the managing of her life and affairs, and of course things like shopping and cooking, which we share. In between these things I have snatches of time where I try to get some work done. So I have enough on my plate to try and keep it all going and should not really entertain the thought of writing this book now. But I simply cannot stop myself. There is a compulsion within me to write this and it floods the page in great chunks. I love writing and it seems that it loves me because with each word that is placed on the page I feel a little bit better and a little bit more clearheaded and positive.

In the first few pages of this book I use the term 'Oh Hell' several times but of course it has a double connotation. At the time when talking to Helen on the phone all those months ago I use the term to show that I was unhappy to be embroiled in this situation. The other connotation is that at times this is Hell. And so the writing really does support me.

I write a blog as a way to promote myself and my writing and below is what I wrote for the last week.

I am back, and sure you think I have been on Walkabout! Perhaps I have.

It's been months since I've been in the bush months with my caravan. I went to South Africa and was to be there for quite some time. However, my father in Australia was rushed to hospital – he will not leave the hospital alive. So I came back to Australia, down in Tasmania, to help out where I could. I have never been particularly close to my father as there were too many incidences when I was a child.

But I was called to help, not by family, nor from some voice from the sky, and certainly not from guilt. Perhaps, more from a primordial force within, a force that called to heal what needs to be healed, to understand more.

Many years ago I gave up the need to forgive my father. What I mean by this is that when there is the conscious requirement to forgive, then that is not forgiveness – that is coercion, or even a lie. Real forgiveness comes from the heart. It is not a conscious act, it just is, and there is no need to feel negative emotion from some wrong that may have been done.

Seeing him, trapped in his dementia, childish and childlike, the fear that used to surround him and govern his ego is stripped. In his incoherent babbling there is innocence, which is more the core of who he really was. And although I don't condone his past deeds, I do not condemn him as a man. Like you and I, he had his demons, but unlike you and I, he did not have the frame of reference from which to grow as an individual. He was a simple man and questioned nothing.

My Dad, is still alive, for who knows how long? But whilst alive, I will sit with him and let the silent lessons wash through me.

Thanks for allowing me the time to go walkabout, but I am glad to be back. I invite you to continue journeying with me, where together we will learn.

Perhaps in time, once this is all over, I will be able to better understand my feelings and the emotions that are coursing through my body at this particular time. Who knows, maybe it's best not to understand at this point in time but to just do what needs to be done, and keep my equilibrium whilst I'm doing so.

4th August

We had a support appointment today with a lady from Alzheimer's Australia who came to check up on Helen. Well she is not actually from Alzheimer's Australia, but a contracting company to Alzheimer's Australia. Her role is one of supporting the client with networking him or her to the various organisations that can help. She herself was advanced in years and hugely experienced in the field.

OH HELL

As we were talking I told her of my concern about not having the control in place to ensure that all medical information came to me. I explained that I did not necessarily want to make the decisions myself as Helen has a brother and sister and other family. But as I was the man on the ground, the person who has taken total charge and responsibility, for the betterment of Helen's future health and security, then it was imperative that I be the conduit from which all information flowed. Her reply was far more encouraging than what I had heard last week. She said that she had a form, that she will drop off, and explained that I would be able to fill out a form for Guardianship of Helen's health issues. She encouraged us to do this.

At the end of the appointment I walked her out to her car to see her off. We chatted beside her car for a few minutes. Looking me straight in the eye, she said, "You know your function here is critical for Helen?" I said I knew that, and she continued with, "Helen is so precarious at this stage… teetering on the edge, that I think if you weren't here she would have slipped over long ago". Tell me something that I don't know, thinks I.

When she continued she said, "Helen has much to be grateful for your support. But it does worry me as to what will happen further down the line when you need to leave".

I then told her that I'm a writer and for many years I have wanted to write a kind of family memoir, as there is much of interest. But now that I find myself in this situation I feel compelled to write what is happening to Dad, and Helen, as well as my own process in this.

She said she felt it would be wonderful for readers to have a better insight as to what does happen to the minds and lives of people who suffer from Alzheimer's, and other forms of dementia, not to forget the anxiety. She then said that she was able to lend me some books from their office library that may help.

Then the conversation turned to Dad and she reiterated what I already knew, where people with Dementia often lose the short term (working memory) but retain the longer term memory. Moreover, what can happen, and this seems to be the situation in Dad's case, is that the memories that come to the fore are those of major events in their life, such as traumas. This could explain his aggression to being handled, as we think that in the POW camp he must have been handled badly.

The results of Helen's MRI were perfect in as much there are no signs of dementia. This should be a cause for celebration, except that Helen is agitated because she can't remember anything, and whether she can't remember because it's Alzheimer's, other forms of dementia or stress, it's all the same to her. Nevertheless, it is a good thing and it does show that there is the possibility of cognitive improvement. But even though she does not have Alzheimer's, I do not believe that she will ever retain her full functionality. The reason why I say this is that Helen seems to be one of those people who just can't handle stress and as a result there will always be a stressful situation, even after my father has died.

In the short time that I have been here, approaching seven weeks now, I would think that she has less short-term memory ability than when I arrived. Of course the stress of Dad's situation will have aggravated her situation but my gut feel says that the deterioration of Helen's memory is more than just stress. In some instances it is so bad that she will ask me why we have a specific appointment at 11 o'clock this morning, and less than a minute later, having forgotten that she has just asked me and certainly not remembering the answer, she will ask me again.

I would think as she gets older and less capable then there will be more stress and aggravation, thereby compounding the memory issue so the future is likely to offer difficulties for her.

Now back to the results of the MRI scan, it is good news inasmuch as she does not have Alzheimer's, which would ultimately lead to an earlier death.

Always at the back of my mind is how much time do I stay here? I do want to help Helen but I have my own life to live and although I'm happy at this time to support and help as best as I can, it cannot go on indefinitely. Helen is the first to agree to this and she would not want me to dedicate my life to her beyond a short period of time. So somewhere along the line after Dad has gone I am going to have to be tough to be kind. What I mean by this is that when I go she will realise how mentally deficient she has become and therefore, she, and only she, will have to make the decision for the next stage of her life. That is; to retain independence but sacrifice aspects of quality of life and function, or moving into a care facility. As mentioned above, we have been down this road and I understand and support her current need to retain an independent lifestyle for as long as possible. However, based on what I see without my support or some other live-in person then I do not believe she will be able to retain that independence for too long.

I have had conversations about this with just about everybody who has some sort of valuable import and some have said what about more support from ACAT, would that help? It would not really support Helen in the way that she really needs it. The only way to really support Helen is by having someone living here on a full-time basis. For instance, let's say she has an appointment at 2 o'clock, and the contract ACAT people had it in their system, and say they phoned her at 1 o'clock to remind her. By 1:05 she is likely to have forgotten that they phoned and that there is an appointment. She forgets, irrespective of how many times it is written and plastered on the fridge and on the table and perhaps even written on her hand. These devices to remind usually do not work and although a message may be seen on fridge the comprehension to take it in is often just not there. And then of course there is the issue of when she has an anxiety attack – for when she is in this state she is even less likely to remember who to phone or where to get the number. So it is unlikely that she would in fact phone them. But even if she did remember to phone them it is likely that that person is not sitting there waiting for Helen's to phone and probably has another client who they are helping at that time. That being that, they would not be able to get to Helen in time to support her whilst she is in that deep anguish – at the time when she is most vulnerable, that is the time when she is more suicidal, and needs them.

With Shrink today, she, after hearing Helen's saying how difficult it is to be with Lou in his delirium, and watching him descend ever closer to death, Shrink asked her, "Do you think he derives benefit from your visits?"

Helen said, "No, not on a conscious level but perhaps on some other level he may".

Thinking about Helen's answer, Shrink continued, "Well, in view of the fact that you don't derive any benefit, and nor does he then I would suggest that you reduce the visits as the visits are so traumatic for you. What I would suggest is that you go in for short periods of time, say twice a week, just to check up on his progress. You have enough stress in your life without increasing more with no real benefit".

Just as we thought the day was pretty much done and dusted, after we had our evening meal, dishes washed and cleaned, the phone rang. It was the nurse in charge of the shift at the facility where Dad is. She explained that Dad is agitated and keeps trying to get out of bed. They are afraid that if he keeps doing this he may fall and hurt himself, such as breaking an arm or a leg (old bones are invariably soft bones). She asked if Helen could come up and sit with him for a while and try and pacify him. I asked her if she had applied the maximum amount of sedative that she is allowed to and she said yes that she had.

So off we went back to the facility to sit with Dad. Once again he had a fixation that he wanted to go somewhere. It was not clear where he wanted to go, and it was not necessarily towards home, it was just 'somewhere'. Helen was not really able to pacify him, and it took all her energy to restrain him, which of course made him angrier. After two hours he did slow down but was still awake, but we took a chance and slipped out back to home and a welcoming bed.

Whilst I was there I spoke to the head nurse and she said that the sedatives that they are allowed to give had absolutely no effect on him whatsoever. I told her that that being the case I will contact the Doctor and ask if he can prescribe a stronger sedative. She then said that his behaviour is consistent with someone who is in pain. He is unable to express it. She suggested to get the doctor to come and give him an examination. This would be good because Dad is even skinnier than he was a couple of days ago.

OH HELL

Lastly on this this, I was proud of Helen. After putting down the phone from the nurse's call, and I told Helen, the colour drained from her face as she realised the difficulty of what she was about to do. But then I saw her take a deep breath and say, "Come on, let's go".

But on the drive home, she said that tonight, restraining and trying to reason with Dad was one of the hardest things she has ever done.

5th August

Within the facility there are other residents, all at various stages of health. Many are bright and still alert and so they tend to visit other residents. That is what had transpired when I came in to see Dad this afternoon. I shall call his visitor Morris.

Morris is big man and must have been a mammoth some sixty years earlier. He is now ninety. But although big he has a very soft and gentle voice with which he chatted to Dad. When I say chatted, it was a dementia's picnic as the conversation was really disjointed and one-way, where Morris projected confusion to Dad, who seemed oblivious to it. But every so often Morris had a moment of clarity. He did when I came in and introduced myself.

We chatted in a simplistic way, about the weather, the food and the like. Dad was a blank witness. Of course as most of the residents are of that age, many had involvement in the Second World War. Morris had, and this was major component of his conscious mind, as it came up several times. He served in New Guinea and had been captured by the Japanese and interned in a prisoner of war camp. There was no indication that Dad was following the conversation. But when Morris indicated Dad and said, "What about him, did he serve?"

For a split second I felt a bit uncomfortable but then said, "Yes he did and had a very difficult time of it". But offered no more.

Morris, not to be side-tracked asked, "Which side?"

When I said, "The Germans, the opposition", there was a hesitation as Morris took that in. But fairly quickly he seemed to accept this as a natural thing and that time has healed and that there was no need for animosity and so nodded Ok in what seemed to be an understanding way.

But I was also watching Dad when I said, "The Germans, the opposition", I am almost certain there was a reaction. He said nothing, but it really seems that this inadvertent barb landed somewhere in his conscious.

6 August

Today we had the first 'Staff to Family member' meeting at the facility where Dad is. There was nothing startling to report at this meeting, other than to say that it went as one would expect, and that they had received the authorisation from the doctor to increase the dosage of medications for Dad, thereby hopefully reducing his irritability. When we commented on this that it would be easier for us, meaning Helen and I, and of course the staff, one of the ladies in the meeting said, "But it will also be easier for your husband".

She then went onto relate stories of how patients are aware that they are agitated and that they don't like being so, and that when they are sedated, it may make them a little docile but it does improve their happiness.

One other thing that came out of it was a confirmation to Helen. They are all aware of Helen's state of health and one of the ladies asked how Helen was coping. I then added that when Helen was at the psychologist yesterday the psychologist had suggested that Helen does not see Dad as it is just too stressful for her. Then one of the ladies spoke up and said, "That advice is more than just sound. That many times family bring themselves to the brink of ill-health as a result of feeling they must sit with their loved one day in and day out. And of course it is worse when the patient is demented as your husband is. In view of your precarious state, it is imperative that you take that advice and limit your exposure to Lou as your first priority must be your own health. We have trained staff and have twenty-four hour attention to him. When he is difficult it is okay for us because we can go home to our families and so it does not affect us but in your case you take that concern home with you. So your number one priority at this point in time is to support yourself".

I am glad that she said that to Helen, and I'm hoping that there are readers out there who also heed this advice. Certainly I will be.

But the question is, will Helen be able allow herself to keep away from him but not feel guilty? Conversely, can she, for probably the first time in her life, consider her own needs and not his? Or could it be that she may think that she will stop loving him because she is not seeing that much of him. Or in return, is she concerned that if she does not visit that he will forget who she is.

The answers to these questions can only be answered by Helen, not me.

7th August

"I don't want to use that thing anymore", she announced at breakfast.

"What thing?" I asked.

"That black computer thingy. It's too difficult."

"You mean the iPad?"

"Yes. It's too complex. I want to work on my old computer. I don't want to get behind with technology. Can you please set it up for me?"

"Yes sure", said I, knowing full well that at this time in her foggy state, trying to re-master the PC is not likely to happen. But I will try anyway.

When she came home from shopping, it was with two large bottles of Olive Oil. When she realised she bought two bottles, instead of one, she was a bit sheepish. But when she went to put them away, she saw the almost full four litre tin of olive oil. "That's odd" she said, "this was not here this afternoon".

Wonder if we can find a use for olive oil on our muesli...

Caregiver... that's what I have become, as I open one of the books that the Alzheimer's lady lent me. I quickly close it. But I do open it again, and read *Alzheimer's Diary* by Mitchell Montgomery. It a great read for those of you who have a love one who has Alzheimer's. When reading it, I think 'You poor girl. You had just what I am going through!' But she does not answer the most important question; is loony contagious?

Today, he seemed even more childlike, with his tantrums, his inane questions in a voice full of innocence, the perpetual changing of subjects, demanding to have his slippers on under the bedding and of course the nappy, which they call a pad. Oh yes, mustn't forget the bib that keeps his brown, check dressing gown cleanish.

"I want a haircut."

"Dad, you had one yesterday."

"Well I want another one."

Is this what he was like at two and a half years of age I wonder.

He then said, "You have big ears" (which I do).

"So do you."

"Do I? Well I'm ninety-one."

Did not know that ears got bigger as we age, but said, "Dad, you are ninety-two, nearly ninety-three".

OH HELL

"Yes, ninety-one."

His next line of questioning was, "Is my lunch ready so I can go to work?"

"It's coming now Dad."

Silence for a short time.

"Why are you here?"

"I am here to visit you, don't you remember me. I am your son Pat."

His face changes in surprise, as if I had said I am a Martian. "My son... you my son?" For a brief time I see his brain exploring this possibility but it's too much for him and the surprise gradually fades from his features. A minute later that surprise and conversation were gone, as if they never happened.

I wonder if he knows his brain is failing or is he is so separated from his mind that he is simply not aware of who he is or was. But if he does have a conscious awareness of who he has been to what he has become, how on earth does his mind cope? It must be like being in a dream, a very powerful dream, where you know you are not the person in the dream, that you are someone other than that person, but you have no control over what happens and so you live as that person who you are not.

For most people, who upon seeing their loved one, perhaps the mother or father, drift further away from their core self, it must be an agonising experience. However, in my case I never knew him well enough to know who he was – an enigma, hidden through silence and misinformation.

Whilst there I went along and saw the head nurse and they had managed to get permission to increase his medication. When I asked if it was working, she said, "Doesn't seem to be as he's still agitated, shouts out, and tries to leave his bed".

I then asked her, "What's that sleeve-bandage on his arm for?"

"He was off his bed and on the floor and he must have scraped his arm on something. There was no blood it was more of a scrape and a bruise. We put that sleeve on just to protect it a bit from getting worse." She then went on to say, that she has applied for, yet again, now for about the fourth time, for the doctor to increase his dosage. She did explain that "the doctor is not keen on doing this because there could be side-effects. But he will have to increase it because (Dad) could do himself damage to keep getting out of bed as he does".

Had a conversation with a friend today on the phone. Before ringing off she asked, "How's your dad".

"Hanging in there" I said, "could be weeks".

She then went on to relate how that, "Just before my brother had died of cancer, and that even when homeostasis was gone, liver collapsed, heart beating at 180BPM that he still hung on. It is amazing just how strong willed the mind is when it comes to surviving, and that it will fight, even when the body function has totally declined". This reminded me of what I said earlier that it seems that we only die when we give up.

And later, another phone call from the facility, this one at 9:00PM.

Just to let us know that your Dad, got out of bed and crawled to the corridor, heading to who knows where. That's where they found him. When I told Helen she just frowned, but to liven it up a bit I said, "Well he walked from Russia to Germany, do you think that an old age care facility is likely to stop him?"

Is it too late to have a second glass of wine?

OH HELL
My Story

This book is not really about me, it is about situations and other people. But I guess I am a major player in it and so aspects of my story may give greater understanding. But I promise you I will not bore you with unnecessary details. My main reason for giving these 'breadcrumb trails' is to give you a framework, reflecting Dad's mind and the behaviour of those of his friends.

Perhaps the first place to start is with the following writing. I wrote this about fifteen years ago and it is been used a few times in different aspects of my writing. The story is true and will help to set some of the scene.

> *My Brother John*
>
> *It was only years later that I ascribed my daydreaming to the German who used to lock me in the dunny for hours on end.*
>
> *Dunny is a lovely Australian word, meaning an outside toilet. This dunny, like all dunnies of the period, was a small hut, invariably made with wooden slats and a tin roof. All seemed to have rickety doors and spider webs in the corners. Dunnies were far enough away from the house so that an incoming breeze would not spoil meals. Yet not so far that it was a trek – who wants to wake up at night, in the middle of winter, and traipse kilometres up the garden?*
>
> *Yes, after Mum absconded, Dad left my brother and me in the not too good care of a countryman of his. I call him the German because, as I was only three at the time, I cannot remember his name. So we stayed with him and his family on their farm out in the back part of Sydney.*
>
> *The German did not like me and took great delight in demonstrating this. One of his favourite pastimes was to lock me in the dunny whenever he went out. Whilst incarcerated, my brother John was given strict instructions not to let me out – otherwise he would regret it. Knowing the German, John was too petrified to buck the command.*

I remember one such time; perhaps it was not just one time but all the times that a small child rolls into one. I must have sat in that box all day. To start with, slithers of sunlight shone through the slats from behind me. Many daydreams later, they were in my face, with dust particles dancing in the shafts of light.

I sat on the closed seat as otherwise, being just a little thing, I would have fallen in. The wood became hard and after a while hurt my bum. Of course, there was no food and no water. I don't recall what went through my mind as the hours passed. I do, however, remember my brother. Not once would he leave my side or rather, the side of the dunny. If I was about three he would have been five. We did not talk, as he was the silent type. But, if suddenly I would say, 'John, are yer there?' there would always be the reassuring answer, 'Yeah.' His support was my solace.

Two hours later: 'John, yar there?' 'Yeah Pat, I are'. He never wandered away or faltered in his vigilance to support his little brother. How my five-year-old brother took on this duty I will never know, but I'll always be grateful. As an adult reflecting on it, I think that in many ways, John's burden was worse than mine.

These memories are my earliest and probably stick because of their profundity.

A year or so later, it was John who supported me while we were in the orphanage. He was my personal guardian angel, always there, not saying much but always a strong presence.

More years passed and he was still there, a silent support system. We grew up and how sad I was when the day came, and as a man of fifteen my brother John joined the navy. He was heading to the other side of the country, some 3500 kilometres away. That was as far away as he could get from Dad.

Now, 42 years later, I still feel the tears prickling my eyes when I recall John aboard a train, called The Spirit of Australia, as it detached itself from the station and pulled him ever faster away from me.

OH HELL

I don't know about the detail but Dad met Hildegard (my biological mother) after the war, probably in Munich. She would only have been about fifteen. From what I understand, her mother (my grandmother) had remarried and saw Hilda as a threat to the new man. Seems to me odd that she marries a man that she can't trust. Anyway, the mother wanted to push Hilda out of the house and so when Dad came he was the perfect ploy. I would imagine that both Hilda and Dad were devastated by the war experience and clung to the other. Whether they loved each other, who knows, but probably so.

I know Dad still had a photo of her in his wallet when I was about fifteen, which was some thirteen years after they broke up. I know this, because he told me the following story.

That she left him, taking John and me with her. However, it was only a few days later he heard a car coming along the seldom-used dirt road and went out to investigate. He saw a car that he didn't recognise stop at the gate. In the passenger's seat was his wife Hildegard. He saw an unknown man, who was the driver and our two little heads just above the window line.

Dad said he was her lover. This was said with real hate. Continuing the story, he said; Hildegard turned around and reached over the front seat to open the back door and shooed John and you out. Our satchels soon landed unceremoniously in the dirt after us. No words were exchanged, just anxious looks. Then the car took off in a cloud of dust. I never saw her again. It was likely that the lover did not want you, nor did your mother.

He told me this story on a Saturday afternoon, which meant he was boozed. It was when he said this that he took out her photo and showed it to me. This was the first time I saw a picture of my mother. I was spellbound, but all too soon he put it back in his wallet and said, but "She got it".

I asked what he meant by this.

"I gave her this good", and as he said this he stuck out his closed fist.

Back to their supporting each other; they both wanted to escape the madness of Europe and so immigrated to Australia. I think John was born very soon after they arrived. Two and a half years later I came along. She was still only eighteen.

As a result of what he had said to me, for many years, I was under the impression that our mother had no interest in John or me. The term 'a crime against humanity' should have been applied against Dad, as I was to learn later, through the sisters (yes, I have four beautiful sisters who I will tell you about later) that Hilda did want to take us but he beat her up and told her to "get out".

Given the damaged minds of these two, it would have been a miracle if it lasted. But of course it did not, and if I am to believe in the following in this would give further indication of how tumultuous their life together was.

Over the years I have done a lot of work on myself to try know myself better, and through doing so to heal those aspects of me where I was damaged. On one occasion I was hypnotised and taken back through various periods of my life and the episode that I'm about to relate was when I was about two years old and just a toddler. The event was where I saw Dad beating Hildegard. In seeing this event, it was played out from exactly the same situation as I saw it as that child. That is, through my eyes and experience. There was screaming from both my father and mother, he in a brutal way, she in fear and there was much pushing and shoving. I could understand that he was hurting her, but I have no way of knowing how badly he hurt her, if in fact he did. Whether he did or did not he was hitting her and she was squirming to get away. It was very ugly. I was screaming and I went over there to somehow make it better. And as I did, in their struggle I was knocked off my feet.

Although it was in a hypnotic state, this was one of the worst episodes of my life because even now I still remember the absolute terror that I felt. I'm not sure why I felt so much terror, whether I was scared for my mother or for my own physical being I cannot say. But I do think it was more the fear of the situation that was hideous. And whilst still hypnotised, after being in that situation, I was trembling all over, tightly curled in a ball and whimpering. When the therapist took me out of the hypnotic state and bought me back to normal consciousness I could not leave as I was shaking so much. It took me an hour for the shaking and the fear to diminish enough for me to be able to drive home. It was the fear of that time that had such an effect on me – it felt like I had been punched in the solar plexus.

I have absolutely no doubt that what I saw in that hypnotic state did in fact occur and the reason why believe this is not so much because of what I saw, it is more from what I felt. That trembling, that fear was too strong to have come out of nothing. It could only have come if it was there. I do not believe a hypnotic state is likely to manufacture that event and specifically those feelings. I believe that the hypnotic state bought out the feelings that were there, as to what I must've felt as a young child. In all probability it is unlikely that Dad hurt my mother badly. There may have been a bruise or two, which is despicable enough, but it is unlikely to be much more than that and may have even been less than that. However, to a tiny child it was a major incident.

I have thought of this incident many times over the years and it is likely that Dad was drunk and it was possible that my mother was also drunk, as she had times where she also relied on alcohol.

Clearly it got to a point where it was intolerable for Hilda to stay in the household. She had to get out and she wanted to take John and me with her. But she could not because he would not let her. He threatened to kill her if she tried to take us, and I believe, that when drunk, he was capable of doing this.

There were further reasons why she was unable to take us. To start with; at that stage she had absolutely no English, whereas Dad had a reasonable grasp of it. He also had a job, and therefore money coming in, which he controlled. She had no job skills or training and so after the war would have found it difficult to get a job. And the last reason was that she knew no one who could really help or support her as all her family were back in Europe. I was told that because of this situation Dad was awarded us kids. So when Dad threw her out with that threat she had no choice but to leave without us. But it was her intention to try and sort her life out and then come back and claim us.

I firmly believe that Dad did not really want John or me but he was not going to let Hilda have us. What makes me believe this is that not long after she had gone, he had literally given us away to those German people, the ones in the story above called My Brother John.

It would seem that we were there for probably about six months until we were rescued by Enid.

I interrupt this transmission with an announcement – will I be there when he dies? Sorry, but I have these interruptions all day. Will he have a moment of sanity just before he goes? Apparently this does happen. I know he does not recognise me since I have been here. Maybe, that he never recognised me! Did he ever recognise John or Steve, or anyone for that matter, other than Helen and Zoe? Normal transmission resumes...

In enters Enid

Enid is a selfless (Australian) woman that came in to Dad's life, and thank God she did. She had recently been divorced and had a child (Keith) who would have been about six. Dad and Enid must have been seeing each other for a while and as a result of that, she learned of us two and wanted to see us. So he organised the one Friday afternoon after his work he would pick us up and spend the weekend with Enid. So there was Dad and Enid, Keith, John, and myself. I do not remember any of this but was told by Mum later. From now on in this story I shall refer to Enid as Mum, as that's what she was.

Apparently for the entire weekend I was reserved and distracted, which Mum thought odd. John, on the other hand was most communicative but was like a limpet and would not leave her side. On the Sunday afternoon they were driving John and I back to the farm, but as we got closer and I recognised the area I started crying. The closer I got the more hysterical I became until as we arrived I was absolutely petrified. Mum is an astute person and straightaway she worked out what was going on.

OH HELL

After Mum saw the terror in me at returning to the farm, she decided to marry Dad. She took control and got us kids away from the farm and those people as soon as possible. She placed us in an orphanage while she and Dad made arrangements for the marriage and to buy a house. We were in the orphanage for six to eight months. I have several bad memories from this time.

But not only that, those German people were returning to Germany to live and had applied to adopt us and take us with them. Mum is Australian, through to the very core, and in her mind there was no way that we Australian kids were going to leave Australia.

Many times over the years I asked Mum if she loved Dad. Her answer was, "No I probably didn't but I did like him and so I thought, and hoped, that we could make a life together and give our kids a family" – and she would always continue, "and there was no bloody way that you kids were going to leave these shores!"

So John and I were taken off the farm and away from those people and put in an orphanage whilst she made arrangements for marriage and a home.

In many respects it is mind-boggling the sacrifice that she made, because if it wasn't for John or I, and the situation that we were in, it is unlikely that she would have married Dad. Nevertheless, a family had been formed and stability gained for the three children. Dad worked, and although he didn't earn much money he was a good and reliable provider. Mum also worked hard, whilst looking after a family of five, especially when she was doing the washing by hand.

I wrote the following many years ago, and it describes the day the family became a family.

When I was about three and a half, John and I were put into the orphanage, there was no love there. It was emotionally cold and barren. I remember the day we were to be collected by Dad and our new mother.

Although little, I remember it like it was yesterday. John and I were pulled out of the hall where all the kids were playing, and given a bath. Was amazing, because the bath was only for John and I, not the hundred other kids as was normal. We were scrubbed and polished – dressed in our only clean clothes and our hair was combed. When ready, we were told to wait 'here', which was in an entrance hall. The floor was, and still is, black and white checkers. We were so excited and could not contain ourselves.

After what seemed like hours, they finally came. They drove a utility, where Mum and Dad were in the front, and two kids in the back. They were big kids, compared to us. John and I were put in with these kids. One of them was Keith, the other was Keith's cousin and buddy Paul. On the way, to where ever we were going, we dropped off Paul. It was a few days after Christmas. But, what was Christmas? I didn't know. I learned quickly enough when we arrived at the house they had bought. The house became a home – 'my home'. It was a strange house because inside there was a tree growing in the lounge! Under the tree were brightly-wrapped parcels. All these years later I still remember what my present was – it was a blue and white speedboat. Later that day we went to the beach for my first swim. The boat came with me. That day is etched into my mind. The sky was deep blue and the sun radiated my happiness. I was with my family. For the first time in my young life, I felt wanted, secure and loved. And it was not long later when a doggy completed the family. (This was about four years before Steve was born)

But this was also a relationship that was held together with sticky tape and wire because Dad was just too difficult. There was also another reason, Mum was educated and genteel, Dad on the other hand was a peasant. I do not mean that in an ugly way but he was most unsophisticated.

There was one glimmer of hope and that was with the birth of Steve. Steve came as a result of their union and for the first time Dad showed a modicum of love towards his new son. But it was not enough and over the years he wore Mum down with his belligerence and his attitude that the male was superior to the female, and that the female must be totally subservient to the male, and to be meek and mild. Well, that would never work with Mum as she was raised in a loving and supportive middle-class house with great education and was taught to be an independent and strong willed spirit.

OH HELL

Through the week, it would have been more tolerable whilst he worked and was away through the day but relatively quiet and sullen in the evening. But on the weekend when often pissed, he was vindictive and unreasonable. This was when he was at his worst and he would give her hell.

The wheels finally came off when I was about sixteen and I had started my apprenticeship as a bricklayer. One weekend when he was drunk he went too far and gave Mum are beating. Fortunately it was not too severe and we were glad it was not worse but she did have bruises. I think the reason why it was not as bad as it could have been was because Mum fought back – "that bastard was not going to hit me".

At the time I was going to teach him a lesson and beat him up (all this is very, very ugly) but Mum begged me not to and the reason was that he knew I would come at him and so he was sitting there waiting with a loaded spear gun (Keith by that time spent much time as a spear fishermen). I also knew that in his drunken conditions that he would be capable of doing anything. So I let it go and between Mum and I we left The Old Man, taking Steve with us and rented a flat. By this time Keith had moved down to Tasmania and was diving for abalone. John, who had to get away from The Old Man, had already joined the Navy.

But going back earlier years, even when Dad was not drunk he was always sullen and distant, and if there was any love in him it was never displayed. Yes, he was softer with Steve but that was about it. But over the last forty years I have seen him with Helen and although he still has the attitude that women must serve the man, he was always soft and gentle with her and did show affection.

The only time that he ever showed interest in anything was when he was fishing. He loved fishing and would fish off the beach with a great big long rod that would allow him to cast way out into the waves. Or he would fish off the rocks. And when there was more time he would hire a row boat and would row out in the waterways of Sydney. He would always take us and although there was no affection he wasn't his normal unhappy self. However, I remember on one of those rare outings that he took us on, I dived off a rock into water that was too shallow. My right thigh scraped along a bed of razor sharp oysters. The cuts that resulted were half the length of my left thigh and the scars are still visible fifty years later. It bled a lot and was painful. Yet, all Dad could say was, "That'll teach you to be careful where you dive".

Although it may seem that my life was one of hardship, it wasn't. After the orphanage we were a regular family – Mum, Dad, Keith, John, myself and later Steve (and always a dog).

As a family we were relatively happy, but there was always tension. Dad never really took to Keith and so made his life a misery. Keith in turn, who was much larger than John I, would bully us for hours when Mum was at work. Fortunately I did not get the brunt of this and John did. But other than that we brothers got on well and saw everything as being fine. Mum and Dad did the best that they could to keep the family together but it was clear that there was no real relationship between the two of them. But I guess the marriage did what it was meant to do and that was to give us kids a home and stability, which it did.

When it was finally over, as related above, it turned out to be the best thing for both of them as they both met and married partners who they were better suited to. Dad met and married Helen, and Mum met Jack and they married. Jack is a good man and adored Mum and treated her with respect.

It was a funny thing, but all of them ended up in Tasmania. As mentioned before; Keith left Sydney and moved to Tasmania as an abalone diver and absolutely loved it. Then because Mum and Jack used to visit on a regular basis they also fell in love with the place and decided to move there. And Dad found his is way to Tasmania as he was offered a job down there. So here I am, here in Tasmania helping out as best as I can.

Back to the earlier days, if we were a happy and relative cohesive family, it was because Mum loved us all passionately and had the ability to make each one of us feel special. There was not much money but we were comfortable. Mum and Dad both worked hard but when not working they were at home and so we saw lots of them. I have many good memories.

It was great growing up in Sydney in the sixties. The house that Mum and Dad bought was within hearing distance of the waves on the beach. And so we became surfies and spent literally thousands of hours down there. John and I were also sporting mad, playing soccer in winter and cricket in summer. These three loves it took up all my time. Keith was not one for sport but as mentioned he loved skindiving, which lead him to become an abalone diver and fisherman. He is now retired and spends about forty percent of his time somewhere between the first and eighteenth hole on the golf course. The other sixty percent of his time is spent regaling stories in the nineteenth hole. He would say that it is a hard life, but someone has to do it.

Steve was not particularly sporty but he loved and still loves riding a surfboard.

Before Author's narcissism, we had one conversation where he pointed out a valid point to me, one that had not occurred to me before. We had been talking about Dad and in this specific discussion I had told him that Dad had never ever shown us love as kids. He never showed any interest in our lives, never asked us any questions about our schooling or sports, in fact he seldom spoke to us. He certainly never hugged us or smiled at us. In many respects he seemed to live in a vacuum and that we did not exist. From our side what we saw was an automation (we would not have use that word as kids but it does fit the way we felt), whereby, this shell went to work every morning, leaving it exactly 7:20. And so he was gone and not really thought about. Then every evening we would hear his car come along the road, change down gear as he went round the corner and then into the drive. There was no real greeting from him and he would disappear into the bathroom for half an hour to shave and clean-up. Upon his re-emergence he would sit down at his place at the table and read the newspaper. We had to be quite, but that probably suited us as it meant it was better if we went outside and ran about, which is what we invariably did. Dinner would come and he would eat his without any real discussion, mainly comments, such as, "This meat is bloody tough". There was never any discussion in the house that I can recall.

After dinner, which always ended at 6:59 PM he would go into the lounge and watch the 7 o'clock news. We had to shut up, absolutely no talking. Then when we went to bed we got a brief handshake from him. Now, being a parent, I cringe at the thought of giving my two children impersonal handshakes. But I guess that is how he was.

The next day, and the other days of the work week were all exactly the same. No chatting to us, no interest in us what so ever. The weekends were different in that he would normally start drinking when he came home from work on the Friday night and he would not stop drinking until Sunday night, when invariably he ran out of booze. But he was organised and never missed work because of booze.

As an adult I can understand why he drank as he had demons to chase. But as a child I did not see this. When he drank he went even more inward and became morose. Normally by Saturday night he would be belligerent and aggressive.

All of this I related to Author, I also said the following;

Watching my father die as I have been doing over these last months I have been told many stories by the nurses that the aggressive and abusive attitude that he has offered is consistent with a person suffering dementia. And they are probably right, but what I see, is what I saw when I was a child growing up – not much difference really.

But back to the comment that Author made – after hearing all of these things he said to me, "As hard as all that may have been, you have a lot to thank your father for". And he continued by asking me, did I have much freedom as a child? "Absolutely," I replied, "we ran wild and sometimes as a young child of about ten on a school night

OH HELL

I might only come home from the beach or wherever I had been at about 9 o'clock at night. Of course Mum jumped up and down but it did not really have that much effect. If Dad noticed, he said nothing or didn't seem to care".

Author then made his point; "That early freedom and independence you had set the course for the rest of your life. You, as I have come to know you, probably have more freedom and independence, and are the most freethinking spirit than almost any person that I know".

Author went on to explain that in his own life, his father, who was abusive, kept Author under his thumb and literally confined to the house. This had the effect of suppressing Author.

"So you see", he said, "that the reason why you have the ability to literally change your life in an instant and embrace something else, if that is what you would like to do, is because of that independent, adventurous and free thinking nature that you developed as that young child of freedom. You are able to do this because you have implicit trust in yourself and there is no fear of consequences. But if consequences occur you have the ability to circumvent them anyway. Believe me, this is a wonderful ability, and one that probably 98% of the population do not have. So not only did your father give you life, he gave you this gift".

Thinking about that then and now, Author is correct. And so certainly I am grateful for this aspect of my character but it could only be at this stage of my life that I would be able to understand this.

Identity – I wonder if Helen has an identity issue that is aggravating her plight. First she was a teacher, but downgraded to be a hobby farmer. Some might disagree with me and think the change was a free move. But then the farm became too much and so it gave away to this little two bedroomed unit in Devonport. Now Dad has all but moved from her life, and so with very few close family members or friends to enjoy time with, I think she is still trying to understand where she is in life… I must try and help her get some friends and grow an identity footprint.

8th August

In tonight's writing I was going to write on another topic, but now that I am at the keyboard it seems that there is another more pressing collection of thoughts that are pushing their way and demanding to be heard. This having to be heard is not only, hopefully for your benefit, but also for mine, as I am still just a child in a sea of emotive issues. It would seem that these need to be looked at and clarified on a regular basis.

For the last five or six mornings when I have woken up, but still drowsy and in bed, my mind has been working out why I am really here doing what I'm doing. After all, as you will no doubt have realised that I'm not all that close to my father; and although Helen is a lovely person she is a stepmother through being Dad's wife.

So why am I really here?

It's funny, every morning when my mind asked this question I already really know the answer, and the answer is that it comes down to the values of who I am as a person.

If I break it down; I am not in the region of the world that I would like to be in at this period of my life. I had planned to spend several months in Cambodia, after spending two months in South Africa. Instead, I came here to do what I felt is needed. But Author was right when he said my life is on hold.

But even with all those impediments I'm still happy. I wake up happy and go to bed happy and I do this because I live happy. Happiness is not something that you acquire as it just is, irrespective of where you are, or where you live. Happiness is not in Cambodia, waiting for me to claim it. In fact, I take happiness with me to Cambodia. We either have happiness or we don't. For those who have happiness they tend to live to a simple formula and they also understand that happiness just is and so they just be it. But for those people who don't have happiness, happiness seems to be a constant fight, it is like the rainbow that is just over there but when you move towards it, it is still just over there, never getting closer. I realised these principles some years ago and so I see myself as a happy person and as a result I am a happy person. Besides, I cannot wait for all of this to end before I am happy again, can I?

Perhaps part of the reason why I can be happy person is because I have clear values in my life, with no blurring of lines. I do not vacillate between one set of values and another. And because they are clear it's easy to make choices without procrastination. And when I do make choices my mind does not concern itself whether the choices are right or not – so there is no conflict within my mind. I either do what I want to do, knowing that it is right or I don't.

For a time I wondered why none of my brothers are here, doing what I'm doing. Or why Helen's family are not here? But I realised I cannot be concerned with their issues or the way that they see life. Nor could that influence me in the way that I see life and what is important to me.

I'm not here out of duty, as duty is anathema to me. All my life I have rebelled against authoritarian figures and duty. If I thought you were interested I could tell you about these. So it is not out of duty that I am here.

So why am I here?

Some might think that I am being a martyr. Bloody hell no, not a chance.

I am here because I know that people are the most important aspects in our life. More important than the money I am losing by being here and only working a few hours a day. More important that being in another country and learning and seeing about the world. It is not about assets, nor career. People, other people, and our relationship to them is the primary purpose of life. It is only through interaction with them can we as individuals be happy. Yes, there are times when it is not ideal, such as this one, but the growth and the satisfaction of life emerges from the good and the bad. This may be considered the bad but in reality it is not, as there is no bad.

And if it is people that give value to our lives, then surely it is family that holds even greater importance to us? As difficult as my father has been, his blood is in my blood. His demons are my demons and my demons are his demons. There is no separating us as we are one.

Helen may not be of the same biological blood, but through the years she has become of the same blood. I could no more discard her than I could discard myself. Or rather, if I did discard her I would be discarding the very ethos that makes me wake up every morning as a happy person. My reason for being in this house and supporting Helen is to give her a window of opportunity through which to grab a better aspect of life. If I can help Helen to retain her independence and dignity, even if only for a year or two then my time here will have been worth it. I have absolutely no intention of dedicating my entire life to making Helen happy, as only she can make herself happy, irrespective of her issues or not. But I do recognise that if she is given a bit of space in which to find herself then this could make the difference to the next stage of her life. She herself cannot give herself this space in this situation, as it is just too difficult for her. But I can give her this space, and I am and I will continue to do so for a time. There will be a cut off time when I need to leave her to sail her own life.

When I received that SMS from Kimmy, and thought 'oh hell', I did not want to do this; but even then I knew that I would as there is no escaping from myself and what is of value in life. Although I delayed it for a week, perhaps to fortify myself for what was to come, I knew exactly what I would be doing. And I knew exactly why I would be doing it. And now that I'm here, and as difficult as it is, I am glad I'm here.

9th August

My son Lance's birthday. Wish I could be with him but alas, South Africa is a bit far to fly this morning. But the Skype chat will be lovely, and I will also get to see my Grandson tearing around the house.

OH HELL

Dad's asleep, mouth open wide enough to drive a truck into it. For times like this I bring my notebook to try and catch up on work. But work is far from my mind these days, and it is this writing that calls me. The words somehow console and soften the current situation.

I look at him and am reminded of the poem that Michelle Montgomery wrote in *Alzheimer's Diary*

> *Old Man*
> *Old man, you are gone.*
> *Your teeth leave your head, but you do not know,*
> *You look at your food as though it is a chess move.*
> *But then you look up and ask,*
> *"Hey Babe, how are you today?" Gone.*
> *Or temporary absent?*
> *Old man.*

I think, are you in there Dad, if so, who are you?

Now that there is no memory is there a you? We become who we are because of our memory. It is the memory that gives us a fixed identity. But in your case, and also the case of Helen on occasions, a concept given three seconds ago is already lost, a mist dissipated in the breeze. Trapped between who you were fifty years ago and this ninety-two year old body.

To remember something is to bring that something to the present tense. And if I was to use an analogy; it is like going and getting a memory from the shelf, on which it is stored, and bring it to our present tense counter. Well that's how it works with healthy people but in both of your cases, two seconds after the item is put on the shelf it disappears... and you are left standing... wondering... ... confused ... annoyed, and you think 'oh dear'...

I might talk about shelves and counters but scientists would talk about synapses. Either way is just semantics and what was there two seconds ago is not to be found. The scientist would also say that the memories are there, it's just that there is no connection that allows it to be grabbed quickly.

And with the memory gone there is no personality. Our identity, which is formed from our memory, and even in some cases is formed from what we thought we thought, and often fictitious, is all that we have from which to draw.

But what about me; if I am the personality that I form from my memories, which may also not always be that accurate, then surely my life is also an illusion. But I, and all of you out there, cling to our illusions, Dad can't.

Helen, the smart girl, has another method to circumvent the problem of the memory not being there – she has me. Often, as we go to the various medical and other appointments, she drags me along, she explains to the practitioner that I am her memory. I am an external hard drive because her hard drive has integrity issues, bad sectors as such. So depending on which sector the data is on, she may or may not be able to retrieve it. Although I always confirm that I am attending the appointments, often she asks me, just to confirm.

Dad's mouth is still open. Half an hour has gone and he has not moved, or made a sound.

Helen returns from visiting Dad, and she is shattered. I'm trying to think of the exact words that she used, but it was something like, "Its horrible seeing him in this state where there is no one home and he is dying. Please, please, please let him die soon".

Another phone call in the night, the great escape continues. These calls have been putting pressure on Helen because she thinks it is another call for her to go and restrain him – she just can't do that too often. When I talk to the carer who phoned, she tells me that it is procedure to tell the family of any incidences.

I say to her, "Please stop telling us, Helen freaks every time. Please continue recording these incidences, and you can tell me privately when I am there. But please, no more phone calls, unless an emergency".

I tell Helen this, and she visibly relaxes.

Shayne

I mentioned earlier that I got some of the information about Dad's family from my ex-wife Shayne. When she grew up with me, she was only sixteen when we married, she always wanted to be seen as being bohemian. But she could never be bohemian as she is too conservative. By the eighteenth year mark of our marriage, she stopped loving me and loved another. For several years after the divorce I hurt badly. But then somehow I swam out of the fishbowl of my existence and into the wide and fascinating ocean and within this multi-encompassing ocean that I have lived in, it would seem that I have become the bohemian one.

Shayne is a lovely person and had a very positive impact upon my life and since the divorce we have both been supportive of each other, in a brotherly and sisterly way. I remember some years ago, at the end of a visit, when I was leaving her farmstead that she and her husband Roy live on, the two of us were walking towards my car and she said to me, "I just want to tell you something before you go: when we were married you were a wonderful husband. And you have been a wonderful father to our children. And for all these years after the divorce you have been a wonderful friend and for that I am grateful". I treasure those words as to truly be a friend to someone is indeed a wonderful thing. In fact, true friendship gives value to life.

10th August

After dusting off and assembling all the components of Helen's PC, I turned it on to get it going. Obviously the agreement for the service provider for the Internet is long expired, and so I go to Telstra and buy just one month of Internet credit. I only buy one month because if Helen does not continue with the PC, then there will be no long-term contract and payment.

But as I start to search the net, one delinquent program keeps loading to the screen, suggestion that it be used. The program is not necessarily an Internet search engine, it's more like some sort of marketing program for selling advertising. 'Eh?' I think to myself, 'what on earth is this?' I then went to Control Panel to see if I could uninstall it but cannot find the program file. I then went to Helen and I asked her if she knew what this was, and after a time it dawned on her as to what happened. Several months ago she was phoned by one of these marketing companies that interrupt our evening meal, and this person offered her, 'Something better' for her computer and so she took it. When I asked her what this 'something better' was, she had no idea. She continued by saying, "That as soon as I put down the phone I knew that I had made a mistake".

Wanting to try and find out what the financial damage was going to be or if there was a debit order I asked her for the latest bank statement but she could not find it.

I will have to phone these people tomorrow and find out what it is and to trying kill the agreement. It would seem that they do this all the time by preying on the vulnerable, which invariably are the elderly – but I have learnt, that an old person, or someone with diminished mental capacity can reverse agreements legally.

But there is one thing that my brain cannot get around and that is, as she had no Internet agreement (I had to purchase that one month) so without the Internet, how did they remotely install this program? I know that there is absolutely no way that she would be capable of installing a program herself. "Damn," I think as I wonder if that phone call Helen took, and the delinquent program are two separate events? If so, there could be two problems to resolve.

All of a sudden he smiles, but just because his face is facing towards mine does not mean the smile is for me – does it?

I wonder if he feels alone in his demented state? Or is he happy with the company that is filling his mind?

Hildegarde's (Hilda) Story

I refer to her as Hilda, rather than Mum to avoid confusion with my other mum Enid. I had been back in Australia for about a year when I received a phone call from Shayne. Her first words were, "I have a phone number". I knew exactly what she meant – that somehow she had tracked down Hilda.

I did not think the number is directly to Hilda, as about five years earlier I had a premonition that she had died. This was strange because I would go weeks without thinking about her, after all she had been gone without a trace since I was about two and a half. Then one day I was working at my computer and suddenly I had an overwhelming sense about her – that she had died. So strong was this feeling that I needed to reflect on it for a time and was certain that the feeling was correct. That's unfortunate, I thought to myself as over the years I often wondered whether I would like to meet her. There was the curious part of me that wanted to – to see my roots, to know her history, to see my biology; but most important of all, who she was as a person. Am I like her? However, the angry part of me, the child within said, not a chance – she damn well did not want me, nor did she ever try to find us, blah, blah, blah... Later I learnt that she had similar concerns... "They", Hilda said, meaning John or me "never tried to find me, so they probably do not want to know me".

Shayne's words bought me back to the present when she said, "I don't really know whose number this is but it should find someone who knows Hilda".

I thanked her and ring off. Stunned, I gaze without seeing out the window. I do not know how long I did this for but I had just been sledgehammered.

For two weeks I sat on it, vacillating between the need to know about her and the fear that kept saying all the blah, blah stuff. I also wondered; that if she had children and if I just rock up and say, "Hi, we shared the same uterus!" What would their reception be? Would they believe me, perhaps Hilda had kept her past hidden and said nothing about John or I. What if she had made a clean break of it and chose to forget. After all, in some ways Dad was her link back to Germany and the war and I am sure she wants that part of her life buried.

Finally, I made the phone call…

"Joe here", said a heavily accented voice of an elderly man. It was soft and gentle in tone. Here goes I think. There was no point beating around the bush and so I jumped straight in. "Good 'ay, my name's Pat and I am a son of Hildegard. Do you know who Hildegard is?"

The ten second silence was endless, I was trapped in no man's land.

After consideration the modulated voice says, "You must be the younger of the two?"

He knows who we are. Surely that must be good news? And I answer, "Yes I am. You know of us?"

"Oh yes I do. Hildegard always spoke of you."

Hildegard spoke of us. I can't believe it. This is the news that I have been waiting to hear all of my life. My throat feels a little bit funny, eyes scratchy.

"I'm Joe and I was married to Hilda for twenty-one years. We had four daughters together."

OH HELL

It's true, I think to myself, there are siblings... but they probably won't be interested in John or me... four of them, my goodness, can't believe it.

"Do you know that Hilda is dead?"

"When?" I asked.

"About five years ago."

My brain said that was about the time I had that feeling.

"How did she die?"

"Lung cancer. But we had long been divorced, about twenty-seven years, and she had remarried someone else. And so did I."

A split-second later my brain says, well she had been married three times.

"It's bad luck your mother is not alive for this phone call. She so much wanted to see you two."

My heart flips backwards, like I'm on the Big Dipper – I like hearing this. Don't stop, tell me again. But he takes the conversation forward, and in his strong accent wanders a bit. I listened ... It would seem that Joe had the utmost respect for Hilda and said many time that she could do anything that she would want to do, but her love was nursing, of which she qualified many years after being in Australia. At one stage, she and Joe ran a roadhouse and restaurant and made lots of money – they sold it and virtually retired. Yes, she could do anything. She was very determined and always successful. As Joe continued, almost as if reminiscing to himself... she was a heavy smoker and died of lung cancer.... but also closed and would not talk about anything that she did not want to. She was the eldest child, born on 22 March 1931.

He remembered her birthday. That, I think makes her an Aries. I am an Aries. Could we be similar?

But then Joe interrupts his dialogue, "Sorry, but I must now go and visit my wife. She is in hospital and also soon to die..."

I feel terrible for having phoned at that time but he assured me, "It's okay, I'm pleased you called. It might be best if I speak to my girls. If you phone me in about a week I will give you one of the numbers".

A week has a hundred and sixty-eight hours but this one seemed to have four thousand or more. I phoned and recognised his voice. "Yes Patrick, I have Jan's phone number for you. My daughters are happy that you have contacted us. I apologise but I must ring off as my wife is very close".

I knew what he meant and wished him well and thanked him.

Although Joe and Hilda had been separated all those years, the respect he had for her came through loud and clear.

Immediately I dialled Janet. She answers, "Jan this is Pat". I then wait to see what happens – rejection or acceptance – love or fear – my mother is not your mother... blah, blah... But I did not have long to wait because the shriek of delight said it all.

Janet is the second oldest, Sue is the oldest, Elizabeth (Liz) the second youngest and Patricia (Tricia) the youngest.

Jan and I chatted for about half an hour, agreeing that we could talk for hours or days and know that we must meet as soon as possible. But before ringing off I asked her, "As our youngest sister is referred to as Tricia, is this for Patricia?"

"Yes it is", she said.

Patricia, the female version of my name. That one hit me right between the eyes.

When we rang off I was totally overwhelmed. A week ago I had no sisters and now I have four and all four seem to want to know us.

From what I learnt, Hilda said nothing about their big brothers until they were old enough. Then one day she explained it all. It must have

OH HELL

taken some time for this to settle into the girls, but once it did, they were keen to meet their bigger brothers.

Next I was going to phone Sue but needed some time to clear my head and come to grips with this amazing phenomenon.

Sue was equally welcoming. She is soft, gentle and loving, more like a big sister to a young brother. I could handle that.

It was Sue who had most of the information about Hilda's early years and so I learnt much about her through Sue. We chatted for about three quarters of an hour before ringing off.

Phew, there are two sisters who want to know us.

At this stage I had not spoken to John about this, but wanted to speak to the last two sisters first, so as to feel the way.

Once again I needed headspace to take in the immensity of speaking to Jan and Sue, and was only going to phone Liz in a few days' time. However, she had other ideas and got my number from Sue and phoned. My head was pumping five hours later when we finally rang off – such was the need for conversation. I had never had such a long telephone conversation, but how does one catch up on a lifetime of events and emotions in a few short hours?

Meeting my sisters was one of the most beautiful things that has happened to me in my life. And also beautiful was knowing that to her last breath Hilda loved John and I. It was later that I learnt that several times she tried to get John and I back from The Old Man. But he always threatened her and scared her away. And then later, probably about ten years later she tried again. At one stage she went through all the Grundkowski's in the telephone book, none of them were us. To her it seemed as if we had disappeared. Of course we had had our name changed from Grundkowski to Grayson. Life can be cruel sometimes.

I was to learn later, that the name change also blocked Zenon (Dad's brother) from finding us as I shall relate later.

In that conversation with Liz she asked me not to speak to Trish for a time, as although Trish wants to speak to me she needs time to absorb this. That was okay by me as I also needed to absorb. But Trish and I start exchanging emails, and slowly we createed trust and a rapport. And then after a time a telephone conversation, and like the others, it was so wonderful.

It was now time to tell John and so I phoned him. "John, I found our mother."

"Good on yah", he says in a noncommittal way.

"She is dead though. But we have four sisters and I have been in contact with them." "What, four... what?" He asked. I knew he had heard but was stalling and so I continued, we are so lucky, "They want us in their life".

At first he was flabbergasted, but then his sense of reality, that is the reality that he had created for himself, kicked in, "Bugger them. I'm not interested and happy as I am without them. They have not been in my life... ever. So why do I need them now? Our mother didn't want us, and made no attempt to contact us. I don't mind if you have contact with them Pat, but leave me out of it".

"John, listen to me, these girls want to know us... they are our young sisters... and believe me, they are genuinely interested. Not just me John, you as well... they want to know about you, not from me, they want to know about you from you. They're reaching out to you."

"Well, let me think about it", and quickly changed the subject, "Did you hear the cricket result..."

So I let John be with this for a time. Four days later he phoned, and in a cautious but firm voice said, "Okay give me the phone numbers".

Later, when I showed Sue this section of the manuscript, she added;

> *I remember you giving me John's number as George (Sue's Husband) and I were heading down to visit Dad not long after Borzena's (Joe's wife) funeral. You told me John wanted to make contact but may not be ready to meet me. I will never forget that initial phone call and how keen he was to meet, said he would be at our Goulburn*

> *motel at three o'clock. Once we met, we were so comfortable together. He checked into the room next door to us and we talked all afternoon, through dinner and again during breakfast the next day. The lovely thing for me was how he and George connected. John had to return home but said he would be at the airport to see us off the following day. How surprised we were to see the whole family with him, even Maree (John's x-wife). Never had such a warm welcoming committee. I'll never forget that.*

From that day onwards John was a different man. Those four girls worked their sisterly magic on him and it was like a light had been turned on in his life. Once he realised that their interest and love for him was genuine he embraced them wholeheartedly and returned the love.

This could not have happened at a better time for him as he had recently gone through a divorce, one that he did not want. But he and Maree had grown apart and it was really the best thing for them both. But at the time John did not see it that way and was pinning for Maree and his old way of life. John now has a wonderful partner in his life and so it all worked out well.

11 August

Well the shopping fiend has struck again. This morning Helen went to the local market. But before she went I made the suggestion that if she saw a nice quiche or something, then buy it for dinner. Which she did. But then at the same time she also saw a nice zucchini pie, which she also bought for dinner. But then this afternoon I went out for a walk and when I came back she was not here. It was not long before she came back with shopping. As she walked in, she smiled and said, "I have a surprise for you I have just bought us a nice cooked dinner".

Well at least we will not starve.

Sitting watching him, watching me, the stare is blank. He's talking the gobbledygook that makes sense to him. I doubt if he is worried about anybody else understanding him or even connecting with anybody else – it is all internal. Some of it is in French, some German, some Polish, some English, and some in Martian.

After a time he says to me, "Who are you?"

"I'm Pat"

"Who? Cat?"

"No, Pat. I'm Patrick, your son."

Thinking for a few seconds, he announces, "I've heard of Pat. I think I know him".

Then silence.

"What is this?" he asked pointing to his watch.

This amazes me as he was always a slave to the time – everything revolved it. I tell him it is his watch.

"Oh... my wife put this on me", he said.

"Which wife?"

"My new wife."

I'm wondering who he means, as he and Helen have been together for forty odd years.

Silence for a while. Then; "what's that?" pointing to the bed (he was in his side chair).

"It's your bed."

"What's it for?"

"You sleep in it."

"Do I? I don't understand."

OH HELL

Silence

"Who am I?"

"You are Lou. Do you know Lou?"

"No."

Silence.

"Shit, I don't understand ... understand anything."

Again he asks, "Who are you?"

When we live in our normal lives our vision is usually external. It's a bit like having a funnel, with the narrow part against our forehead and the wider flange reaching to explore the outer world, that is; everything that is within that wider world, people and politics; all our issues, our needs – all receive that focus.

As modern humans it is important that our view is external, as that is how we grow. But mostly we are the central player in that view. All of our thousands of monitored and unmonitored thoughts are about how we look in the eyes of that external world – do we look good?

Dad's view on the other hand is where the funnel is reversed and that the wider view is focused inward and the narrow view is being made smaller and smaller and so that there is virtually no external view. There is no outer anything. His new view must offer an entirely different perspective. I wonder what that perspective is?

As humans we grow through exploring, via the wider end of that funnel, but his time of exploring is gone. Or is it? Could it be that he is exploring a frontier that I do not understand? Most of the doctors and carers would say that there is no exploring going on inside that head, but who really knows?

When I get home it is perfectly obvious that Helen had been crying and anguished. Before I can say anything she bursts out, "I have been sitting here frantic that I have not seen my husband. Nobody will tell me not to see my husband. Nobody will tell me what I must do or what I must not do. I don't want anyone in charge of my life".

"Helen, nobody told you that you can't see Lou. It was only a suggestion and these were made by Shrink and also the head nurse at the facility. In both instances they made the suggestion because they can see that you do not cope with visits to him and that your state of mind is more important".

"I don't want to discuss this anymore, I'm going to see my husband and nobody can do anything to stop me." With hysteria she heads out the door to go and see Dad.

As she cannot remember the head nurse or the psychologist making those suggestions it is obvious that she thinks that I told her not to see Dad. At first I'm a bit pissed off but mollify myself with a deeper understanding of what she's going through. I also remember what I wrote earlier that it would be interesting if she would be able to let go – she can't.

Two hours later she returns, even more anguished and with her soul-wrenching fear apologises (at least she remembered the bollixing she gave me) and says, "When I go I get stressed. But if I don't go I also get stressed – what can I do?"

Meeting the sisters

Now that John was entranced, as we all were, a three day weekend had been arranged in Brisbane. Trish and Sue both live in Brisbane, and at the time Jan was living in Mackay, and Liz down at Coffs Harbour. I was floating around as I seem to do, and John lives in Canberra.

With anticipation John, I, and Belinda (John's daughter) landed at Brisbane airport. We knew Liz and Trish were going to be there to meet us – both had taken the day off. Sue, a teacher, would come through to Trish's house after school and Jan was to fly in the next morning.

OH HELL

The euphoria of seeing my sisters in the flesh is beyond words. The English language is not rich enough to adequately express the feeling of seeing these girls and to hug them in greeting. I will always cherish that moment, as I will, the moment with Sue later that afternoon, and again with Jan the next day. Once again I say, without a doubt the meeting of these four beautiful siblings is a highlight in my life.

It was not only four new sisters that came into my life, it was all their husbands, their children and their children's children, all of which amassed to about thirty people. And my mind is still being boggled ...

For that three-day weekend we were inseparable and did not stop talking. We talked in groups and we broke off and spoke to each other on a one-on-one. It was not just about getting to know them as people, and them wanting to know about us, it was also about them telling us what Hilda was like as a person, her strengths and weaknesses.

The talking continued ... she has my chin ... I have her eyes. Jan and I look more similar. But there was one common trait that coursed through our conversations, one that any external observer would notice – we are loud. All of us are loud. Even Sue, who has a soft and gentle voice is loud. How charming to have a family trait. Of course there were more, many more.

We all have weaknesses and it would seem that Hilda never tried to hide or make secret of hers. What she was was what she was, and that's what she expressed to the world. But it would seem that her overriding goodness and generosity and love for her children and life, her exuberance and adventurous nature out shone any issues that she had.

All her life she had goals and things to do and things to create. Like everyone, she had her failures and her successes but she had the ability to see the good in everything and just keep going, irrespective, to finally succeed or to move to the next challenge.

It did not take long for Sue to assess my character, and so said to me, "You are probably more like Mum than any of us". She was referring to Hilda's ability to be happy with her own company and wanderlust.

Hilda smoked all her life and had and on occasions drank more than was good for her, which apparently worsened after her divorce from Joe. Some of the sisters told of some very uncomfortable times of their childhood and as young adults. These are not my stories to tell you, they are theirs, and so I will not elaborate, but needless to say Hilda could be difficult at times.

The following gives a short account of her days in war torn Europe.

She was about eight when the war broke out and it did not take long before hardships were part of the daily grind. Living in Munich, life was very hard for all, especially young Hilda. Being the eldest sibling she had more chores than the younger children and was forced to grow up quickly.

Munich in the early days of the war, and even prior to the war, was known as the centre of Nazi growth. It was here that Hitler set up his headquarters. It was also here that the Nazis opened the first concentration camp at Dachau, which was on the outskirts of Munich. Sadly this was one of the worst concentration camps.

Later in the war, the city was bombarded with about 170 air raids. So bad were the bombings that about a third of the population left the city. But sadly for Hilda and her family they stayed and endured the worst of it. Hilda found it hard to cook a decent meal as there was only one pot in the house, the rest taken by the military to make planes and ships, etc.

My Grandfather, Johann Schutz, managed a theatre, or was the caretaker, and the family lived at the theatre. Hilda would have been about twelve when the Brits dropped their bombs. The family would take shelter in the basement of the theatre as the bombs destroyed life and limbs above. In 1945, when she was about fourteen, the Americans captured Munich, and also liberated the concentration camp at Dachau. Hilda worked in a chemist shop for a while and saw photos taken by the American soldiers of the bodies piled high in the concentration camp.

OH HELL

The damage to Munich from the bombing was massive and ninety-five percent of the city needed rebuilding. But buildings are easy to replace, but how could the inhabitants rebuild their damage lives?

Further aggravating the situation, Hilda's father died in 1943 when Hilda was twelve years old. Sometime later, her mother Antoinette remarried a younger man. Clearly her mother did not trust her capacity to retain his interest and Hilda always felt that she was in the way. Years before, Antoinette had organised for Hilda's younger sister Margot, to go and live with an aunt, her sister-in-law Annie. So it was at that time a relationship between Hilda and my father was encouraged. A marriage quickly followed and subsequent migration to Australia. Hilda was about sixteen.

It would have been this horror that both Hilda and Dad wanted to escape. Neither ever returned.

When Hilda wanted to leave Dad she had no money and so moved in with friends that they had met. They were more Dad's friends, and not her friends, but she had nowhere else to go. These were the Germans in the dunny story above, the one's Enid rescued us from. In fact, they were Austrian but I thought they were German. But not having any money, Hilda had to leave us kids with The Old Man until she organised herself. It is possible that John and I spent some time with Hilda living in a room at the Austrian peoples' house. The Austrians were buying a farm (probably the one we were on in the story). At this time Hilda managed to secure a job at a factory in St Marys (Sydney) and so the Austrians said, "You help us financially and we will build you a cottage on the land". So for a period of time (I don't know how long) she gave them virtually all her small wage. The mother must have baby sat John and I while she worked.

Apparently Dad came every weekend to visit Hilda, always with a male friend (perhaps to intimidate Mum?), never alone, demanding he have us boys. Hilda was frightened and during one of his weekend visits there was an altercation and Hilda had to leave (this could be the one that I saw when under hypnosis).

The following is also from Sue; Hilda, realised that the Austrians were never going to honour their promise, and so moved into the house of some Czech people who became friends (these people remained family friends for years). Through these people, Hilda met Joe, who was working at Brookvale in a brewery.

Your dad's visits, and his aggressive nature, caused problems with the family and it appears your Dad's demands just wore her down. From what I gather Mum and her friends thought Dad would tire of the responsibility of having you two boys and after a week or so would bring you back. But obviously that didn't happen and he applied to keep you, or so everyone thought (but I have absolutely no doubt that Dad did not really want us, it was just to spite her).

As Dad applied for possession of John and I. He told the authorities that Hilda had abandoned us, had no job or money. No doubt he told them other things as well, but he never would have told them of his beating her. The dumb bastards believed him and so he got the 'rights' to us.

No sooner did she leave, that Dad gave us to those Austrian people. It transpired that they had asked Dad to organise the paperwork for adoption as they wanted to take us back to Austria. The mere fact that Dad gave us to them and that this conversation took place shows just how much Dad wanted us. But Joe told me that they had absolutely no want or interest in us, and that is probably why they treated us badly. All I can say is thank Goodness for Enid's intervention.

According to Joe, Hilda was petrified of Dad, as he beat her once and was continually threatening to do so. This I had already learnt, from Dad himself.

So Hilda, wanting to be far away from Dad (by this time she had met Joe), went north in NSW and started a new life. (Before she left the area she often thought about kidnaping us, but learnt that she would be jailed if she did).

At one stage her mother (Antoinette) came to Australia and whilst here, visited Dad to see how us kids were. He would not let her in, and also threatened her. This of course is all very different from what Dad told us.

Joe said, that later, there were many times Hilda wanted try and get us and was desperate to do so. But life was against her. He said that Hilda pinned for John and I. So distraught, she ultimately tried to block it out of her memory and could not bring herself to talk about us. Every time Sue or Janet (being the older two) raised the topic, she would get angry and tell them she did not want to talk about it.

With the sisters, we spoke numerous times about Hilda's death and the time and the events leading up to it. Liz is a practising nurse and was with Hilda when the diagnosis of lung cancer had been given and that Hilda only had a months to live. As they walked out of the surgery, and in a small sad voice, Liz asked, "Mum this is terrible. What are we going to do?"

Hilda was quick to say, "I think we should go to the bottle store, buy beer and have a party".

Liz lived nearby and was there to help and support Hilda through the following eighteen months, and towards the end moved in with her. The other sisters came and supported their mother through chemo and periods of hospitalisation. Family, and friends visited Hilda during that eighteen month period. And at the end days, all came and shared, as they did at the funeral and afterwards.

We should have been there.

It is now about four years since that stunning meeting with my sisters, and the learning about them and their life as children growing up with Hilda and Joe. It took quite a long time to absorb all of this so as to be able to chisel out the personality as to who I felt Hilda was. The following thoughts are my thoughts, and not those of my siblings. When they read these words they may not agree but they are my impressions. So here goes ...

I do not believe that Hilda ever recovered her emotional equilibrium after the horrors of the wars – a child growing up with bombs and hardship. And then the emotional rollercoaster of Dad's brutality and losing her two boys as a young mother, never to see them again.

There were periods of time when she drank a lot, I think it was her support. As writing helps me makes sense of life for me, her drinking softened some of the difficulties she had undergone. And then of course the smoking. All smokers know the risk and all have a choice to give up or continue. I think that Hilda's smoking and drinking, virtually to the end of her life, was not necessarily a death wish, but more of a bargain, where she bargained with her horrors to leave her alone, irrespective of the final outcome, which of course was death. She loved her daughters and was probably, but subtly, proud of her achievements. And of course she loved her grandchildren. But there was that ledge in her mind that was stocked with pain. The booze and the cigarettes would never win over the pain but it would allow her to get on with life by masking them. It is likely that in her intelligent mind she knew what the ultimate consequences could be and it would seem that when these consequences emerged she accepted them as reality.

I started to write this this morning, and now at 4PM, the day has been swallowed up in the blink of an eye, hardly noticing that it has gone. But I have left one of my favourite memories of the story of finding our mother and sisters to the last, and it goes like this… As Hilda was dying, she collated a few mementos that she wanted to give to John and me. She gave them to Sue and said to her, "One day you are going to find your big brothers. Please will you give them these? This one is for John, and this one is for Patrick". They were like the little satchels that a loving mother would hand to her child when the child is about to head off to school. There were all sorts of things in them that were important to her. But the best for me was the quotation that was beautify scripted in calligraphy by Hilda (another one of her talents). The quote, I think it was from Dr Wayne Dyer, but I can't be sure but think its origin derives from a Celtic poem or writing… and it says, *May you always find new roads to travel, new horizons to explore, new dreams to call your own.*

Reading this quotation, as I often do, brings me as close to Hilda as I could possibly be. I am also cognisant of what Sue said to me that she felt I am more similar to Hilda's character than any of her children. For good or for worse, thank you Hilda, so bring it on.

But I am still not finished. At the time, knowing that John and I were to visit the sisters, they, beforehand went through their photo albums and selected specific photos of Hilda and themselves when they were growing up. They bought frames and lovingly placed each photo within the frame to form a collage of wonderful images.

Both John and I treasure these and they are proudly displayed on our walls.

I have learnt a bit more as to how to help Helen in her difficulty. She easily gets overwhelmed, for instance; if three letters come in the post on one day, she has difficulty. She is OK receiving one a day, but three spark a short in her brain. Not sure how the post service will handle any instruction to only deliver one letter at a time, and hold over additional letters for days when there is no mail.

If I need to discuss things, it is always better to only discuss one at a time. If I discuss several things, one after another, this also blows the circuitry. It all becomes a jumble in her brain. Helen's logic still functions very well, and when she understands something, and remembers that something, she is able to reason things well. In fact, her deductive powers are astute. But the information must go in slowly, so it can be grasped and managed. This is a bit like factory workers working at a conveyer belt when someone increases the speed faster than they can process the items. Helen's conveyer speed process was excellent when she was younger, but now the conveyer needs to be slowed, then slowed again, and then slowed some more...

So it is, little information in at one time, let this be processed and understood. Then later, at some other time, give her the next chunk. But when receiving information, not just from me, often she will say with firmness, "Stop, please give me that again, but slowly". I have learnt to recognise this need and so do as she wants.

Zenon's Story

Zenon was Dad's younger and only brother. By all accounts, even though four years different in age, they were close and liked each other as children. Years later, Zenon often mentioned his love for his big brother. Yet, Dad did not show the same sentiment.

But with the war and then after the war there came a separation – they joined different sides, Zenon for the US Airforce (but this was towards the end of the war), and Dad for the Germans. Zenon is dead now, and also died of Dementia.

When the Germans overran France, Zenon was only twelve and too young to be taken. I am not sure how he and his mother Alfreda fared in the war. It was late in the war that Zenon received sponsorship from a Polish (family friend) gentleman for him to go to Chicago, IL, USA, where he later enlisted in the US Air Force. This however, must have been a real turn-around, as Marcel said Zenon as a boy was a member of the Hitler Youth Party. This is understandable, as according to Marcel, the entire family were Nazi loyalists. But I would suggest that as a young boy he was influenced accordingly, but has he matured he formed his own mind and changed alliances. Because of Zenon's linguistic abilities (French, German, Polish, Russian and English) the Air Force transferred him to Germany. This was in the early days of the 'Cold War' and espionage was heightened. He was assigned to intelligence to interrogate the 'left overs' from the concentration camps in Germany. One of the camps, Dachau, which as mentioned before was just outside Munich. It would seem that he was there to see the bodies being taken out. But before, when working in the area nearby he asked a local, "What is that horrible smell?"

"It is the Jews, they cooked the Jews", he was told. The smell never left him.

As a side note; As Hildegarde was from Munich, and as Dad could have been with Hildegarde at the time, it is possible that Dad and Zenon were in that city at the same time without knowing it.

OH HELL

It was also in Germany, possibly Munich, where Zenon met Wilhelmine Brandl who he later married.

After the Berlin Airlift was over, they, Zenon and his new wife, were transferred to France. It is unknown what his duties were in France or if he remained as a CIA operative. In 1953 they had a child Stephan Grundkowski (my first cousin). In 1954 they were transferred to Colorado Springs, Co. to attend flight training/Para trooping school. In July 1955 their second child (Chouch) was born. Then another transfer returned him to Germany, this time to Frankfurt. Once again his duties here are unknown. But I was told that Zenon had occasional trips behind Russian lines (remember he was fluent in Russian), but was very tight-lipped as to any of his activities. In 1960 he returned to the States, to Virginia, but four years later he returned to Frankfurt. In 1970 he returned to America and remained there. Of my grandparents, Wladyslawin and Alfreda, they survived the war and visited America in the 1960's. But later Alfreda was supposed to have committed suicide.

As mentioned above Zenon was in Germany after the war, and supported the effort of the Berlin airlift. In case you have not heard of this, here is a quick overview.

The Berlin blockade commenced in nineteen forty-eight and continued for about a year. It was one of the first initiatives in what was to be become known as the 'Cold War'. After America had occupied their portion of Germany, including the portion that was to be known as 'West Berlin', the Soviet Union, occupied the rest, wanting all of Germany, including West Berlin, as one of their satellite states. To disrupt the American effort of supporting the West Berliner's, the Soviets blocked all access to that part of the city. They did this by manning blocks on road, rail and the canals. To overcome this, the Western Allies organised an airlift to freight in supplies and food. This was a massive undertaking as the population of West Berlin was large, requiring 9000 tonnes of supplies each day. This necessitated over 200,000 flights.

Zenon, who by this time had achieved the rank of master sergeant E-8, which was as high as an enlisted man could achieve. He was ambitious and wanted to become an officer and so to improve his educational level he enrolled at the George Washington University and was accepted to study there (I could not find out what he studied). Later, the military invited him to study further and become a lawyer as he had ably proven himself in court with many of the cases he had worked on. But with a family and his normal job he was too busy. It appears that not all can get into George Washington as the entrance qualification is very difficult so he must have been smart.

According to Patricia the last of his three wives (a very sweet lady who I had many calls with) said Zenon communicated very little to his family about any of his history or his clandestine work with any of the agencies. Yet, according to her he was so gentle, for instance; he could not hurt any animal, would not shoot a dear. He passionately loved his two children, and was a wonderful step father to Patricia's kids. And, with a smile in her voice, she told me that he was the love of her life.

At one stage she told me that Zenon played guitar and said in her strong Southern accent "When we were a-courtin he would serenade me". He apparently would correct her English, and so she would make up a word and slip it into the conversation. He would pick it up and say, "You're fooling with me – that is a made up word isn't it?" She giggles at the recollection.

He loved America and by all accounts was a good citizen. He loved country and western, saying that is was 'grassroots' America.

When I asked Patricia about Zenon and Dad's mother Alfredia, Zenon said she did not commit suicide, she must have been killed. Apparently, she worked against the Russians (the capacity of this work was never given, perhaps underground, or perhaps an activist) and Zenon felt the Russians 'knocked her off'. Zenon made mention of a letter that Zenon received but this was never seen by anyone in the family.

No one seems to know how long he served as a CIA operative but the Cold War was known to have started around 1947 and endured until 1990 so it could have been for some time. But when the Cold War was starting to dissipate it was suggested that he move into the Federal Bureau of Investigation (FBI) for drug enforcement.

When he retired it was to the Mississippi area where he and Patricia purchased a new house. Sadly they was in the path of Hurricane Katrina (2005, with over 1800 fatalities) and the house severely damaged. Although he was not physically damaged in the storm he was emotionally affected, his dementia deepened and never recovered. Zenon died in 2005 at the age of seventy-seven.

Zenon came to Australia several times as part of his CIA activities. Each time he came he tried to meet up with his elder brother. But alas, he could not find us because of our change of surname. Apparently, he even asked some of his colleagues here in Australia to look for us but of course no one thought of a name change.

Digressing for a minute. It was Enid who said that it was Dad who explicitly wanted the name changed, and his reason was that apparently he suffered bullying when in France as his name was foreign. So he did not want us kids to suffer in the same way. But the cynic in me could suggest that he did it to lose any trace between the Grundkowski in France and himself.

I have spoken to Dad a couple of times about Zenon and he was disappointed that he never saw his younger brother again, after 1929. I am also disappointed because I would have liked to have met my Uncle. It would have been good to fill in some of the gaps. But I also would have liked to have met him because he sounds like a fascinating man.

He is buried at Sandhills State veterans Cemetery, North Carolina, where he had a full honorary military funeral with the twenty-one gun salute.

A few years ago I was at a book festival and spoke to one of the other authors there. He was an ex-CIA operative who had retired and written a book on the subject. When we chatted I mentioned Zenon as they probably would have been of the same generation. He did not know Zenon but when I asked him that if I was to write to the CIA (whereby I would explain that Zenon was my uncle and that I would be interested in learning about him), and would this be a good idea. He said that; they may not reply to my letter, but if they did they may not tell me anything. Or if they did make a statement, the statements may not necessarily be all encompassing. He felt that I would be wasting my time to try and get information. I heeded that advice and so I have let it go. But over the years, through Shayne, I have had contact with Zenon's daughter Chouch, who has been kind enough to tell me what she knows. One thing she said, and said several times, was that her dad was secretive, and like my dad, said very little of those years.

12th August

This experience means that more dynamics build upon me, whilst some of the previous dynamic fall off – a kind of evolution if you will, thereby rendering me a better and stronger person. Every experience, every thought, emotion, and weight of seeing things has built, coral like, one polyp on another to make the new whole. Each polyp an experience, to grow the coral head, or a growth in my life.

I like this analogy with the coral. Where I see bigger, better and brighter colours than perhaps those are displayed in previous times.

I then wondered if this process that I'm in and this change is preparing me for my own pending old age? That change is also likely to be reflected in greater compassion for the elderly and the infirm, the sick the disabled, which is something that I did not have in any real detail.

Life is the most wonderful teacher if we allow it to be.

This morning, like other mornings, after about thirteen hours of sleep, she wakes up at about nine, has a shower, breakfast and washes up. She then heads to the couch for a sleep. She usually also has a sleep after lunch, and often just before our evening meal, especially if I'm cooking, which is about five nights a week.

At breakfast I was watching her and had a premonition that there is something further wrong with her health than what I have spoken about earlier. Because of her illness she is sickly thin and frail, but what I see is more than that. Something else has developed that I feel is more than just her previous ill-health and the current stress she is undergoing.

Over the years I have come to trust my intuition, like that time when it told me that Hilda had died. I think to myself that I must watch closely to see if I can pick up any symptoms from which might support her medical practitioners with a diagnosis.

14th August

Being Friday, Helen has had the appointment with the contract ACAT lady. As usual I don't participate in this as I want Helen to create the rapport with the lady. I want the lady to get to know Helen well enough that she can be in a position to monitor her. There have been about four meetings now and I'm wondering about the efficacy of them. This lady comes in and is bright and chirpy and usually dominates the conversation. Other than a quick, "Hello how are yah", all discussion is normally about herself, the client's she seen, the shopping she must do, and yes, taking the car through the car wash and many other day-to-day issues.

I do appreciate that much of the conversation must be social exchange, and social exchange is good, but as she does most of the talking, with Helen sitting quietly, hands on her lap and politely listens, with the odd, "Oh yes", or, "Is that so", then how does she evaluate Helen's state of mind? I really think the lady needs to be able to drill down into Helen's mind, to see what's going on there, to see if she is coping or if there are new issues. I would have thought that this process would be the most important part of the entire visit but this does not seem to be happening.

At the end of this fourth visit, I asked Helen, "What do you think of the lady?"

"Well she's a friendly soul, don't you think?"

I then ask her if she thinks she is deriving any benefit of this lady coming and chatting?

"Probably not," she says, "but it is nice to chat to her".

I think to myself that I will leave it one more visit and if I still feel the same after that visit then I will make contact with the management and express my concerns to see if they are valid.

But Helen sort of pre-empts it by stating, "I don't want those people coming here anymore. They don't help me".

I make a mental note to phone the coordinator on Monday.

15th August

A two glass of wine day today. Helen bad, Dad bad.

Helen had the worst and longest series of panic attacks today since I have been back. They came in waves, about five of them, all lasting about forty minutes. And when in these, every minute or so she would be 'jolted' as if she had been given an electric shock.

I'm out of my depth here.

Went to see Dad to see if the medications had been increased. No they hadn't. Apparently the staff had a hell of a time with him last night. He hit one nurse twice, which was hard enough to hurt her. He also hit others. He swore, spat and shouted for constant attention. When I was there he was agitated and also shouting. Needless to say I did not stay for too long.

This afternoon I'm feeling great when I consider the support from my family and friends. What triggered this appreciation was a call from my friend of twenty-five years, Tersia. She is from South Africa. She called to asked about Helen and I tell her, "Helen has been part of this family for forty odd years. We have a massive debt to her because it is she who took The Old Man off our hands, hallelujah". She laughed.

John phones me about every two or three weeks to see how I'm going and how is Dad, as do many of my friends, and of course Mum does. All understand how difficult this situation must be.

Often when I am talking to the carers or nurses at the facility, and when specifically talking about Dad's behaviour, many of them say that that is part of the dementia process. But today there was one nurse who may be a bit savvier than the rest. She tentatively asked me, "Has your dad always shown signs of arrogance and self-centredness?"

I am glad that she felt comfortable enough with me to say that and of course she was right. There is no doubt that the dementia is driving a lot of his behaviour, such as the anxiety and the fetishes to do things, with the constant need to get out of bed and go anywhere, but without a doubt there is an underlying trend that has run through his life, she was clever enough to see it for what it was through the sickness.

16th August

We are at the hospital – not visiting, but in it as Helen has cracked.

The depression, the stress, the anxiety finally broke her. The waves of anxiety that I mentioned yesterday were worse this morning. So bad were the electric-shock like jolts that I had to hold her in the chair otherwise she would be catapulted to the floor. The current attack has been going on for about two hours and so I took her to emergency at the local hospital.

After one quick look at her they took her in. At first they were worried about seizures, but I knew this was not likely.

The shocks seem similar to the Tourette's symptoms, and so as I sat in the waiting room I Googled Tourette's. I learn that what I have been calling electric shocks are part of the Motor Tic disorder (sudden, rapid, non-rhythmic movements). Although it is not Tourette's Syndrome, I can see that her Tics would be of the chronic range when at their worst.

Today's episodes commenced where they left off yesterday and in between the waves she was so remorseful that she was suicidal again "...what do I have to live for... the garden does not make me happy any more... life is so horrible... when is Lou going to die? ... there is no point me living..."

I kept trying to convince her that after this is all over that she still can have a good life, but this does not help her at this time.

She also kept referring to herself as being stupid, with the allowing of these jolts to happen to her, blaming herself as her fault. I remind her that depression is a disease and can't be helped. I continue by saying that the stress of Dad's condition and behaviour exacerbates the depression and the depression deepens the stress.

"I know", she says... "but I am so stupid, why can't I control this... I wish I were dead..."

OH HELL

Sitting in the waiting room there was a young girl, about nineteen who was having a loud cell phone conversation with a person, who was probably her mother. I did not want to hear her conversation but could not help it "...Well it's yar fucken fault I left home... yah bitch, yah just coulden stop whingin..." This went on for about twenty minutes until she shouted into the phone, "Fuck off, I don't need yah", and gratefully there was silence where she or the mother must have ended the call.

Gawd, I think to myself, life is just too short to live it like that.

The doctor finally sees Helen, another newly arrived Asian. A nice young girl, who seems to be carrying her own stress. "Hew long heve these been going on?" she asks in a heavy accent.

"Beg your pardon", said Helen, "can you please repeat that"

She does and this time we understand her. "About an hour", Helen says.

I interrupt, "Three hours now Doctor". "They heve taken bloods and results very normal. Vat medication are you on? Did you bring them?" I answer this one as I know Helen would not remember. "I did not bring them as there is quite a long list. Can you not look on the system?" (the system is an Internet based patient database, where all medical practitioners login and access the patient records).

"Oh yes, very good ting. I will do dis."

She then disappeared for another half an hour. Upon returning she says, "I hev made a recommendation to your doctor to for heim (the doctor is a she) to set up an EEG, vitch is a brain vave scan (an electroencephalogram – detects the electrical activity in the brain). I vink dis es a good fing to see".

I make a mental note to phone Helen's doctor on Monday. I also think it would be good to get her to see Shrink again, and ask her.

She then gives Helen a Valium and half an hour later the motor tics slow and finally stop.

Driving Helen home, she says, "We didn't need to go to the hospital, I feel so good".

"Helen, it is because they gave you a Valium." I hope the Valium lasts for hours, no weeks, thinks I.

17 August

I just had a call from John to see what the latest was. After telling him as to where Dad is and the difficulty with Helen, there was a silence for a time, then he said, "It would be so much easier if he just died. He has no quality of life and it would be best for him if he went. And I can't understand why they keep him alive, they should just let him go".

"Of course you are right", I said, "and that is what I've have fought so hard for, that they don't keep him alive any longer than his natural body would have. But you have to understand the people who are caring for him are carers and they will do the best that they can to help someone going, and if that means extending their life because they gave him an antibiotic for an infection, then that is what they will do. The line of help and support, or the extending of life is not always a distinct line and so I can understand that it is not easy for them; and even though it has been documented by myself and also by his attending doctor, there could be times when that mandate is not adhered to".

I went on to say that the reason why the doctor is reticent to increase Dad's medication to pacify him a bit more is that one of the side effects could cause a stroke. That stroke might reduce his life by two weeks – and duh… he is nearly ninety-three and dying already. My

OH HELL

belief is that the doctor would probably be prepared to authorise a drug more readily if it wasn't for 'the system', whereby he would rather be cautious to protect his back than to do what everybody agrees is in fact the reasonable thing.

I also received a phone call from Shayne today as she wanted to see how I was getting on and what the new situation was with Dad and Helen. We chatted some time when I told her that I was writing this book. She is delighted and we started chatting about the material that she had collected and was to email this through. So now my inbox is bulging with all sorts of sorts of 'family-tree' stuff.

To give her an idea of what I was writing I cut and pasted the above section on Hildegard and sent it to her. This is what she wrote back

Dear Pat

It's beautiful, made me cry several times. Very special.

Thanks for sharing I feel blessed to have brought back some love and forgiveness and happiness to your beleaguered family (from her research and finding Hilda).

Love
S

Spoke to the night shift of the facility this morning and Dad worked his way off the bed twelve times in the one shift. Of course being the middle of winter, here in Tasmania it is freezing. Once he's out of the bed it only takes for a few minutes for him to get very cold.

Hooray, Shrink listened to my plea to give Helen Valium. The same as the one they gave her at the hospital last Saturday. It worked really well and so this could make a big difference to not only Helen's life but mine as well.

Since the last one wore off, the poor old girl has had a terrible time with the shuddering and those tics but I had to wait until today

(Monday) to get her in to see Shrink. I am sure that for the few months, until Dad finally dies, and things settle down after the funeral, that she will not become addicted. She does not have addictive behaviour patterns in her life and as far as I know has never had an addiction. The other thing is that I now know how often she must take these and in what quantities and so I can monitor the process. What I am also hoping is that if she settles a bit with the Valium, then it is possible some of her cognitive function and memory may improve, as there will be less stress.

I also discussed the recommendations to Shrink, as made by the doctor at the hospital on Saturday. "No need," said Shrink, "just a waste of time and money".

Today Shrink said to me, "I must thank you for your help with Helen. Your intervention in her life at this stage is invaluable. I shudder to think how she would be today if you weren't around".

Twenty minutes after I got the prescription for Helen, she took one tablet, the first smile broke out for a day and a half. Thank God.

Dad was crawling around his room like some sort of crazed animal. Pants discarded, but with the big nappy on. The door was shut to keep him in and to muffle his shouting. Dad has always been a tall man, but after having lost all that weights, and has he flayed there on the floor, he reminded me of a large praying mantis.

But a clever move, the staff put a mattress on the floor, adjacent to his bed to stop him from hurting himself.

The doctor finally approved of the stepping up of the sedation to Haloperidol, which is supposed to help with psychosis. He was on Risperidone for the same reason, but the side effects are not good. They have also put him on Ordine, which should help with any pain that he may be experience but at the moment it seems impervious to him. So we start the process again, please increase again. Apparently they are going to try another brand, a new product.

18th August

Helen is floating around like an angel. How nice. But she feels that one full tablet is a bit strong and so tomorrow we will cut it in half and see how she goes. Funny, half the population of Australia are looking for the floating feeling, where the other half avoid it.

And although the shaking and shuddering has decreased, it does not seem to have any effect on her depression, which is always worse in the morning. I guess there is no silver bullet for everything in conditions like these.

20th August

Disaster. Helen woke up a complete mess with an anxiety attack that had reduced her to a quivering wreck. She shuddered herself out into the kitchen where she came to tell me that she would rather stay in bed for a time longer. I agreed and said that I would get her breakfast and bring it in and also feed Zoe.

What happen to the Valium and why did not work, I wondered. She assured me that she took the full tablet as she was supposed to. To crosscheck this, I counted how many tablets had been taken out of the plastic holder. The tally was correct and so I could not understand this.

She emerged about three hours later much improved but still shaken. Throughout the course of the afternoon she gained her equilibrium and got through the rest of the day okay.

21 August

As I woke up I was most interested to see how she was, fortunately she was her normal unhappy and depressed morning-self. I say fortunate because it means that perhaps the Valium has worked properly this morning, not that her normal morning depression is a good thing.

Thinking about yesterday's aberration I have come to the conclusion that somehow she mucked up a tablet. It could be laying under her bed somewhere after having fallen off the table or some other reason that made her think that she had taken it. I make a mental note to keep checking the tablet container to monitor if there is one less tablet in the box per day. Even so, there is no guarantee that she had taken the tablet.

At breakfast this morning we chat and I tell her that I will see Dad later today as I've not seen him for a couple of days. For a time she is quiet and then said to me that she just can't face seeing him like that. She then went on to relate how hard it was for her as a teenager to see her mother reduced to much the same state as Dad, and that when she goes it will traumatise her.

I sympathise with her and remind her that her visits to him do absolutely no good to him and that it is pointless upsetting herself to the degree that it does.

Later, after replacing her tracksuit house clothes, for her 'outing clothes', she said, "I'm going into town to replace my watch battery. Do you need anything?"

"No thanks. See you when you get back."

OH HELL

An hour later she comes in and said, "Look at my new watch band. Isn't it nice?" "Yes", I agreed. "And did you manage to get the battery for your watch?"

"Oh …I …I …I can't remember. Did I get the battery, now let me think? I don't know."

"Well look at the time, is it correct?"

She did, and said, "No, it's dead. I must have forgotten. Oh well, I'll just go back to town and get it done".

Other Resident's

After having been in the facility fifty or so times, I recognise many of the residents who are not confined to the beds or rooms. The oldest is 107 and what a spritely man he is – and still driving. Imagine being 107 and with your memory intact. The changes he has seen. This man has his own unit and still cooks for himself, and often cooks cakes for other residence to enjoy at afternoon tea.

There is another man who must be about eighty and is as mysterious as his blank stare. The poor man was found in a caravan out in the sticks, and so no one seems to know his history.

The facility block is a square, with some rooms on the outside of the corridor and rooms on the inside of the corridor. And so if one starts at a point in the corridor and keeps walking, soon enough they will arrive back where they started.

Another man uses a wheely-walker but the walker is a tall one, and so the man stands almost at full height with only the slightest lean on it. Irrespective of the time of day or night that I am there, I will see him circumnavigating the block. As he walks, it is with hardly any perceptible foot steeps, more of a slight push as he silently propels himself along the shiny vinyl flooring. It's a bit creepy seeing him floating along, galleon like, majestically sliding along without sound or movement. Adding to this, is the expressionless face that glides past Dad's room every five minutes or so. Most of the time he sails clockwise but occasionally his travels are anti clockwise. Around and around, travelling past the door, like the sweeping second hand of a watch.

When I pass him I nod or smile, but the blank stare seems to comprehend nothing, other than one more circuit.

Joe is demented and worse than Helen, but not that much so. In periods of lucidity he says, "I never wanted to end up in a place like this, going loony and watching my marbles roll out the door..."

And I witnessed a conversation with one poor old soul and a nurse, where the old lady told the nurse about an intruder in her room, "where this horrible man went through my cupboard and took my purse". The nurse, feigned horror and said, "My goodness, how horrid. I shall go to the office and call the police right now." Apparently this conversation was a regular occurrence and each time the nurse said her bit the patient was much mollified and asked, "do you think they will arrest the man?"

And then there is a poor old lady who lives down the corridor who is hanging on at the behest of her selfish husband. This lady has a throat reflex, where her throat muscles are no longer working and so she cannot swallow. If this old lady had her own way she would have passed on some time ago. The husband who has guardianship over the wife, refuses to let her go and so she is fed through a pipe into her stomach. She is bed bound and has absolutely no quality of life. But there is worse, the husband has a liaison with another female resident and so he spends much time in her company and in her room. Of course our poor old lady she knows this but has no control over the situation.

With each passing day I am more and more convinced of the need for euthanasia. If I was that poor old lady I have no doubt that I would have wanted to end my life, and removed the feeding pipe. And what of the husband, what right does he have to keep her under those circumstances?

OH HELL

A friend told me how her father, who was in deep dementia, as to how he would fight the reflection in the mirror. Every time he saw that man staring he would snarl and shout at him to get away.

22nd August

"Good morning Helen how are you today?"

"I would like to ask a favour of you", she replied by way of a greeting.

"Of course what is it?"

"Can I move back into my old bedroom? I just don't feel comfortable in that room of his, I can't sleep in there. It just does not feel right."

Jeeze I think to myself, first we moved her in there, as that is where she wanted to be. A week later we had to rearrange the furniture a second time, which took the best part of two hours. Then about a fortnight after that she was not happy and wanted to rearrange the furniture again, which ultimately went back to what it was originally. And now she wants to move it all back and into her bedroom again. "Of course Helen, shall we do it after breakfast..."

A night of respite was wonderful, as Deborah invited me and one of her girlfriends to dinner. She made a salsa, salad and prawns for main course and a trifle for desert. I supplied the wine and Jan, the other girl, brought a lentil curry.

As I have mentioned earlier, Deborah is a carer and a nurse, and so she does shifts at the facility that Dad is in. By now Dad recognises her and sometimes he is nice to her and at other times he is not. When he is not nice Deborah is firm with him but also very caring.

She told me the following story. Last night she was at the facility and went in to check on Dad. It was his normal demented self that greeted her and so she attended to him as needed, but just as she was about to leave, it was as if a switch had been thrown and all of a sudden there was a difference in him. Looking at her he said, "Tell Helen that I love her". But then, according to Deborah, with desperation he grabbed her wrist so that she could not leave, and then this time said in a louder and firm voice, "I want you to tell Helen that I love her… I love Helen. You tell Helen I love her". Only after he said it about eight times did he let her hand go.

Deborah reads tea leaves and does the tarot and so my fame and fortune have now been assured, what a relief. It was a good and entertaining night with lively conversation – just what I needed.

23rd August

This morning at breakfast I related to Helen Deborah's story of last night. I knew that it would upset her. But I also knew I had to tell her. I knew that she would cherish those words to the end of her days – they would give her strength and support over these coming weeks. I also know that she will remember them.

After telling her, her head dropped to her chest and there was absolute silence, other than a sniff or two. I left the room as I felt she needed to be alone.

It took her three hours to compose herself and when she did she knocked on my door and asked me if I would mind driving her to Elizabeth Town, which is about fifty minutes' drive. There is a pub/café there that she and Dad used to go to for coffee and cake as an outing. "Would I mind?"

How could I refuse, cake I mean!

Ensconced as we were, at the table in the cafe, with a window seat that overlooked a wintery stream, and green rolling hills. Cows grazed, totally obvious to us, whilst the farmer worked on his fencing. It was pleasant and serene.

Helen had Chocolate Brownies and memories. I had carrot cake and the same story told four times. But it was a much happier Helen as we drove home. She was chatty and intelligent and related many stories to do with all the farms along the road. Perhaps the most interesting one was a farm that had been run by a family, where some fifteen years ago they planted an apple orchard only to learn that that parcel of land gets saturated with water. And so after about ten years they pulled out all the trees and let the cattle back in.

I received an email from Shayne asking me if Dad has a birth certificate in the house, as this would help her in her research. The following is my reply to her.

> Hi Shayne
>
> I asked Helen and she does not remember seeing one. We then went to the old cake tin that he uses to store his papers, there was virtually nothing in it. Not even immigration papers. He may have lost these things over the seventy years since the war.
>
> However, it is possible that he never entered Australia with one. To do so may have meant that he would have had to carry it on his person, for not only the duration of the war, but those years after the war and in the refugee camp. I think his survival would have been more important to him than the survival of his birth certificate.
>
> I would think that he would have been given a temporary ID document when about to leave Europe for Australia.
>
> Pat

Zoe's story

Zoe is of an undeterminable breed. But somewhere there was Labrador. Yes, she may be a pretender to the breed but she has many of their traits, one which is gentleness.

Now you may be thinking that my writing today has reached the bottom of the barrel. But I can assure you that she's probably the most intelligent and interesting of all of us in this household and so needs her place in this missive. But she would have us think that she is central to the household and that all others revolve around her.

Anyway, back to her traits. The main one is that she is a food seeking vacuum cleaner of a dog that would probably explode before stopping eating if given the chance. The daily meals last just five seconds (she has two meals a day) and then it is back to her position in front of the heater, accompanied by a loud but satisfying snore.

What about her intelligence you may ask?

Well how was this; she has the cunning to head outside each morning, walk around to the front of the house in search for a rolled up newspaper, which could have landed anywhere. Once found, she claims it with her mouth and trots with much pride to bring it to Helen in the kitchen, thereby dropping the prized possession at her feet. For this amazing intellectual and physical feet, she require a treat in the form of a doggy biscuit. Me being slightly cynical, wonders if the daily demonstration of intelligence and endurance would continue if there was no culinary delight at the end of it. I somehow think not. A pat on the head is not likely to cut it in her mind.

But, as you will soon see, it could just be that everything does revolve around Zoe, as she has one very important function in the house, and that is – to keep Helen sane. The walks that they have together are probably the most therapeutic part of Helen's life and do far more than all her doctors and medication do. Often, when in her most foggiest of times, that walk brings clarity and calm to Helen.

Zoe's effect on Helen extends beyond the walk. When Helen watches that brown, solid, and snoring doggy on the floor, I can see that it is a major comfort to Helen, especially now that Dad is out of the house.

May you live longer than most dogs Zoe as you have work to do.

OH HELL
24th August

Was a whacky day. In the afternoon Helen informed me that she was going into town as she had some things to buy.

Will you do some shopping? I asked as I went to check the refrigerator. It was as bare as Mother Hubbard's cupboard.

So off she went and returned a couple of hours later. I was working and so did not pay much attention when she came in, but at dusk I went to check what she had bought. And as I did she said to me, "What time are you going out tonight?"

"I'm not going out, what made you think that?"

By that time I had open the fridge door and saw that it was still as bare as Mother Hubbard's cupboard. I then asked her what she had bought for dinner and she replied, "I bought myself a chicken drumstick".

"Helen, did you buy anything for me?"

"No. You are going out tonight."

And so, as we say in Africa, I had to "make a plan" and scrounge the cupboards for something to cook.

A bit later, I was looking for a grater and could not find one in the normal places. So I went to a cupboard that was seldom opened. When I did there was quite a strong smell and upon investigating I found a bunch of bananas. Of course we always put bananas in pots in cupboards that we do not go to. Helen had no recollection of buying them or putting them there, but it must have been a few weeks ago because they were rotten.

27th August

Dad was much quieter today and hopefully it is the result of (at last) a change in his drugs. They have introduced a new drug (Trazodone), which is a sedative and also an antidepressant, whilst increasing the Ordine. He was less agitated and much more settled in his behaviour. But there was still not one sentence that he put together that made any sense, and seemed that he was a little further into delirium.

Sitting there, I had this image of his brain and imagine the plaque spreading like mould across old cheese, ravaging his neurons in a barbaric quest. With each neuron claimed another light goes out upstairs.

One hundred years ago they would have said he had senile decay and two hundred years ago they would have called him mad. Such a terrible disease... yesterday I read that in Australia one person is diagnosed with a dementia of sorts every seven minutes.

It is possible that his more moderate behaviour, coupled with seemingly increased dementia could be a result of some of the morphine based medication that they are now giving him? This raises a moral issue in as much as, should he be given these morphine based drugs that manipulate his behaviour, or should they be withheld? In theory, the answer to that question should only be given by Dad, but as he is unable to form an opinion or to express any formed opinion then his management team, including me, must make that decision on his behalf.

As he seems more settled and less agitated then I would think that including these medications is the right decision. I think a calmer demented mind is better than an agitated demented mind. But certainly, without the agitation he is less likely to hurt himself through his wanting to get out of bed and roam the facility.

Nevertheless, it was an easier visit.

OH HELL
26th August

I have now been here long enough for the winter garden to become a spring garden. To see the drooping heads of the Daffodills overlooking the lower plants in Helen's garden. The pansies with their wine-red flowers, the Irises, white and tall. Grey winter days are slowly being usurped with warmer blue-skyed days that allow the headlands far up the coast to be seen with crystal clarity. Snow can easily be seen capping the hinterland ranges and I feel that more will arrive before winter draws its last breath.

Over the many weeks, routines have been formed and a new way of life lived. Within that though, I am trying to maintain a moderately normal working life. Previously I would start work in the morning and continue through the day until it was time to knock off. But in this situation, work time is broken up into, grab a bit of time here, and so I work in spasmodic chunks.

As mentioned before, I am writing much of this manuscript in the early hours of the morning, or whenever I can. It amazes me as to how the writing of words cocoon's me from living in this looney-bin of a life. It seems that with each placed word and each new sentence that some of the stress and the aggravation flows out of me and into the ether.

You often read about how psychiatrists are among the most vulnerable for their consistent daily contact with people who have mental issues – often being affected themselves. Could it be that my being ensconced in this mental institution will affect me? Thank goodness for this writing, and if not one other person reads the final product, it still will have been worth it.

I also wonder about Helen as to how she will cope after Dad's gone. Although she has been diagnosed as dementia free, I think there is more to her deteriorating condition than the stress. Today I am going to set up a full medical for her as I do not think she's had one for some years. Maybe something will emerge as a result of this.

Today I spent time on the net trying to determine what happens to the brain when the brain is exposed to long-term stress. What I learnt was not encouraging and confirms my suspicions.

The quick answer is that long-term stress kills brain cells. In the short-term the body can handle stress, and with good reason as this supports the survival process, in fight or flight response when perceiving threats.

When stressed, the brain releases cortisol and too much cortisol has a damaging effect. Studies have shown that having prolonged levels of cortisol destroys cells in the hippocampus and there are strong indications that chronic stress causes premature ageing of the brain. The hippocampus contains that area of the brain that is responsible for episodic memory.

Excessive cortisol for long periods, binds to the receptors inside the neurons (in those cytoplasm), and the result is that excessive calcium is released into the membrane. When neurons become overloaded with calcium, they fire less frequently and also die.

In addition to this, excessive cortisol in the blood is a cause of depression. Some neuroscientists and psychiatrics are now suggesting that the major changes in serotonin and other neurotransmitters as seen in depression are not the cause of depression, but are secondary to changes in the stress response. This possibly answers the question that I have asked all along; did the depression cause the stress, or did the stress cause the depression in Helen? Certainly, both aspects would have contributed to Helen's cognitive dysfunction. But it would seem, based on this information that Helen's stress is the main contributor. And there is no doubt that the stress is what caused her digestive issues, and once they came, the stress increased.

OH HELL

This is cause for concern because I believe that Helen has a low stress threshold in as much as stress gets to her more than perhaps other people. Then as she gets older, her stress is likely to increase even more. At the moment she is on Mirtazon, which is an anti-depressant, but this does not seem to eliminate her depression. It is possible that she would be far more depressed if she was not taking this or some of the other depressants, as it is not decisive in its effectiveness.

So unless Helen can control her stress levels, and unless the antidepressants work better, then I can only see her slide continuing. And if there has been damage, as caused by long-term stress, then that damage cannot be reversed, so even though she does not have dementia in the technical diagnosis, she still has a mental and memory frailty that is unlikely to improve. In fact, it is likely to get worse.

29th August

It takes Helen about three hours to be fully conscious once she gets out of bed in the morning. She is like a wound down clock where the second hand sweeps ever so slowly. She is dopey and muddled as she plods inefficiently around the kitchen compiling her breakfast. Fortunately her seventy-three years have programmed her to do this by remote action.

Once awake, the fixations kick in. I see in her the same propensity to fixations as the Old Man and the resident who circumnavigates the ward a hundred times a day, or Dad, wanting to get onto the floor. Her latest is to clean the fifteen metres of concrete path that starts at the back of the house and goes down the side. For the last ten days or so she has been out there, for hour after hour, with a high pressure hose, flooding the concrete into submission. However, the difference between before and after the clean is not all that obvious, even though a dam of water has been used. Nor was the path really dirty to start with. Yet her stubborn determination holds no bounds.

I say nothing and am pleased that she is active but it is a concern that the fetish is often about non-relevant tasks.

The fetishes are not important, what is important is that I try to get her to focus on the good she does. That although there seems to be cognitive damage, there are still millions of neurons that are still firing. I try and get her to focus not on what she can't do, but to focus on what she can do.

It is this reason why she needs to stay in her home for as long as possible, because when she goes into a facility, the focus changes to – you are here because of what you cannot do. You are here because there are too many damaged brain cells.

Her abilities may be diminishing, but the essential Helen is still in that emaciating body. She still is the Helen character in her brain, even if dysfunctional. There is still the capacity to love and support, to be of significance. And she still has an identity, not flawed, but strong and vibrant.

These are the things that she must know. Yes, there will be adjustments on the way, and it is likely to get harder, but Helen is a fighter and she will fight this every millimetre of the way.

30th August

Sitting in his chair, he is much quieter today. Always disjointed in thought he seems happier.

And I think: you have confused me today. You stopped us from being with a loving mother, but you gave us away to the Austrians. You murdered our cat and were often callous and belligerent. You beat up both of my mothers. You did more, much more than what I have related in these writings. But out of all those things the worse by far was that you showed absolutely no interest in us. We kids could have been Autumn leaves that had blown in through the door, of no consequence, and soon to be swept out of the way.

But today you placed your hand on my knee and patted it affectionately. I'm bamboozled. Did you think I was Helen or perhaps John at that moment? Was there intent behind the gesture or were you just living the hallucination of your disease. But there is no doubt about it, there was affection in the gesture and if those synapses unexpectedly fired correctly then who was that gesture for?

The term passing over is an interesting one. In Dad's case the passing is slow, like he is on a conveyer belt heading towards that unknown door. The conveyer belt is running at slow speed, and each day you are closer to that door but not there yet. I can see the differences in your physical body. Little tell-tale signs of you passing on but only when you get to that door will you have passed over or passed away. What I am really getting to is that the process is underway, where the conveyer is heading only one way, and once on the conveyer it is only a matter of time.

But I also see the changes in the persona at it passes from man to cadaver.

2nd September

Fortunately, not much to report on with Dad over the last few days. But when sitting with him yesterday I remembered his crest of Poland, of which I have not thought about some forty-five years. The one he had was made of pewter or some such alloy and so did not have the colour, other than a grey metal colour. The crest, usually of a White Eagle on a red background, depending on which era as different eras have different representations. He had his placed on the mantel piece in the lounge room.

I am trying to get to understand his patriotism or lack thereof for his country of birth. If he went as a volunteer to Germany, and long before he would have been called up, in support of the German cause, as Poland was in invaded by Germany, I wonder how well this sat with him.

It is unlikely that he would have had the Polish coat of arms if he had no affinity or liking for the country. And then there is an interesting tradition with his Christian name, which is Lech. Lech was the 'legendary' founder of Poland for the Poles were known as the Lechites. In the legend, there were two other brothers to Lech. These were Czech and Rus. The myth tells that the three brothers, who were on a hunting trip, followed different prey in different directions. Lech went to the North, Czech to the west and Rus to the east (Russia), where each settled in those respective territories. Of course there are many versions of those myths.

If Dad's parents were German sympathisers, it strikes me as ironic that they gave Dad that name with all its symbolism. And then there was his interest in Australian soccer, which in those days the major league teams were representations of European clubs, and so Dad's team was the Polish team, which was called Polonia. I went along with him on a few occasions to watch and in those games he would be happy if they won and annoyed if they lost. Yet he never spoke to any of the other Polish supporters. Nor, as a child growing up did he ever speak his of birth country, but remember he was only about seven when he left Poland. In fact, I don't think he ever went back.

I could have starved today. At the normal time Helen came to me and asked me if I would like her to cook dinner tonight.

"Yes please", I said. So I continued with my work and every so often I could smell aromas emanating from her effort. Thinking that it must be about ready I went into the kitchen to get mine. Helen was already seated eating hers. I thought mine must have been in the oven. But the oven was off and decidedly empty.

"Where's dinner", I asked.

OH HELL

Looking stupefied and embarrassed, she said, "I kept thinking that I'm forgetting something, and couldn't work out what it was".

Just as well that I like eggs on toast!

When my eggs were ready, I sat down to eat as she finished hers and so we chatted. The conversation drifted on to the fact that I would love to see my new grandson in South Africa and his big brother.

Wanting to be helpful she said, "I don't mind, why don't you take the car and go and to South Africa. How long do you think you would be away for?" I thanked her for the offer and said I would take it up in a week or so.

I have started the process of the full medical for Helen. Bloods and ECG were done the other day. Bone scan appointment set up, as is a breast scan.

Another issue that I have noticed with Helen is that as her form of dementia deepens, and as the long-term memory box gets eaten into, that things she could do before, such as change a battery, are harder now. The memory as to how to do this has receded, and the logic with it. What was once easy is now difficult, or virtually impossible.

Over the last two days Helen has had a break from the concrete cleaning. Good thing, as she has been at it for two weeks now. Yesterday, she went and bought pots for pot plants, nine of them. She had a place in yard to fill and wanted three tiers of three pots. For a time she could not figure out how to elevate theses so asked me. I was glad to help and within a time we had worked out support for the back and higher row, then the middle row. The first row to sit on the ground on a board.

Next, she filled the bottom of the pots with stones, which is the right thing as it helps with drainage. Then not being happy with the potting soil she fortified it with nutrients. Off again to the nursery she bought the plants. All of this was done with confidence. One small error. The plants were a mixture and some were marked down, which tickled her as she does like a good bargain. But these plants, when I surreptitiously checked, were winter plantings and we were now in spring.

Nevertheless, I am sure that with her loving green fingers, that in time that corner will have a wonderful profusion.

The main point though is that she still has the capability to conceive an idea, plan and then expedite it.

Today I learn that a symptom of dementia is one of wandering. Usually there is a purpose to it, such as going to a previous house that was lived in. So it is possible that Dad's persistent want to get off the bed is for that reason. Except that he has not been able to walk for months.

Daylight saving started today. This posed a real problem, as at first, clocks were put forward, then back, then back further and then forward. Every few minutes Helen came to me and asked, "What is the time?" There are about five clocks in the house and so she went to each and made the adjustment. Once again, one went forward by an hour, and another backwards by two hours. But finally, she got them right.

It would seem that as Helen's dementia deepens, her understanding of cause and affect diminishes. Today for instance, I was sitting outside on the bench in the spring sun going over a manuscript that had been sent to me. In the garden it was pleasant. But Helen came and sat beside me on the bench, which was fine until she started running a steel brush through Zoe's hair brush, where fine particles of hair floated in the breeze all over me. I think for most people this would have been obvious what was happening but in her case it just never registered that there was an issue.

I did not say anything as I did not want to offend her in any way, so I just said, that it was time to go inside.

But then an interesting thing happened, I heard the voices of young girls who were probably from a Christian group and they paused outside the fence, which is only about six meters from where Helen was sitting. At first they admired the garden and had a little chit chat with Helen, and then I heard one of them say, "We are talking to residents and we are asking them what they like the most about their life." There was small delay while they waited for Helen to answer, and when she did it was loud and unequivocal. She said "the most important thing to me is love". I was amazed, especially when I remembered what she said to me that day about nobody has ever shown her any real support until I had.

It's funny, when I come and sit here, with Dad, it is when I do most of the thinking about this stuff.

Earlier I spoke about Dad's memory not holding anything on its shelf. I also drew a comparison that it is from our memory that our personality is formed – no memory, no self identity. Recently I read, that some Yogi's teach that a lapsed memory is the equivalent of self non-existence. I'm not sure that I agree with that because a lapsed memory does not mean a mind that is not conscious, but it is an interesting thought. So if his memory is not functioning but his consciousness is, what is going on in there?

But there is more; we are creatures of habit, and habits help to perpetuate our personality. Habits give direction and form to our life. The alarm goes off at the same time every day, year in and out. We tend to shower at the same time every day, pour a glass of wine at the same time, and so on. For Helen, she would be in more of a mess if she did not have habits that tell her, now it is time to feed Zoe, or herself.

Now, in Dad's situation, one by one his habits have been stripped away. A few new habits have been instituted by the staff in the facility, but they are not his habits, so they don't count. And now, he has not one habit left. This is even more removal of his identity.

And what about his perception? It's gone, or certainly blunted because there is no short term memory from which to hold the thought (the perceived idea), and so it is gone before he has time to consider it. After all, perception is a formed idea. So this means the poor man is never likely to perceive many things again.

And if you think about imagination, expectation, anticipation and even illusion, all are based on memory, and if the memory is dysfunctional, then surely so are all of these?

And as his memory is virtually non-existent, then there would be no future in his thought process. Any projection of the future, must be based on things in the memory; such as, I need to go to the shop. The reason for going to the shop, say for eggs, is because the information that there are no eggs can only be stored in the memory.

As a kid, occasionally I would come into contact with some adult who recently returned from some far away country, China for instances. This person would try and explain the exotic nature of the land. But as a child I could not even hope to imagine what it was like. It is the same with Dad's mental state. So I'm wondering what's it like living in the middle, where there is no past, and no future.

Perhaps I think too much.

8th October

Today Steve my younger brother, and his son Ben drove up from Bicheno to visit Helen and also to see Dad.

Was great they came, not from Dad's point of view, as he did not have any idea they were there. But it was great for Helen's sake as she needs to know that family cares.

OH HELL

Certainly Steve was not prepared for the Dad that he saw. It was a far removed version of the one that he had last seen some four years earlier. It only lasted fifteen minutes – that's all Steve could take. Dad was awake and less agitated than normal, but totally incoherent.

10 October

On my visit today I bring my notebook so I can work if he is sleeping as I need to write my blog post. Being here it is natural to look around and take things in, and what I write is not necessarily what I have taken in in this visit, but perhaps all visits all rolled into one.

These visits have influenced me on how I think about life and the three main periods of life. Here is what I wrote:

> *The newly born, middle years, and old age.*
>
> *When you were born you did not care if you were white or black? Nor did you care if you were not white or black?*
>
> *When born, you had no hate but you were smart enough to learn it fairly quickly.*
>
> *Nor did you worry about money. But as you aged you learned to be in fear of not having enough.*
>
> *Were you concerned with your appearance, or rather, did it worry you if you did not look good in the eyes of others? The truth is, you didn't give a damn! When you were born you were less complex and knew what you wanted. Your mind was not cluttered with numerous things because your focus was always on one thing at a time. When you wanted food, you only wanted food. There were not ten other wants cluttering your mind.*
>
> *When you had food in you, were dry, and not tired, you were content – there was no scheming for more – nothing was missing – no greed or need for excess.*

When you fell over, you got up. There was no moaning, you just got up – there was no aggravation – you got up – and let it fade from your memory. It was only later that you learnt to hang on to aggravation.

At that young age the thing that drove you was wonderment – all was exciting. It still can be.

A child is not stuck in one direction – it is happy to change direction at any time, and is able to let go.

A new born does not strive for identity – she is enough.

At that time you did not think you were better than others. Nor did you think they were better than you – can anyone be better than anyone else?

You were not afraid to learn and learn you did. It was later in the class room where you compared yourself with others, where you learnt to be small.

When did you come to the conclusion that you were not good enough? When you were born you did not think this, so when did you decide you are not perfect just as you were?

So what happened to you – from that excited, adventurous and fearless child?

Influence happened. You were influenced by people and society. And that was when you stopped trusting that you would receive.

For your first years of life you trusted that all your needs would be supplied. You knew food, warmth, comfort and love would be there. But somewhere you lost that trust.

And now you are old.

Your life may not be great, but you get on with it.

In your middle years, your biggest enemy was influence. Now you don't give a hoot.

Your younger and middle years may have influenced how you felt about white or black? Now you are more willing to put your hand out to a white, black, or yellow.

When born, you had no hate but you were smart enough to learn it fairly quickly. When old, you are likely to not be bothered with it. You have learnt to just be as you are and let things be. You understand that everyone's journey is difficult, and frankly, you have enough of your own issues to fill your mind. So good luck to you, whatever colour you are, you say.

You may not have much money. But as you aged you learned that normally you have enough to get by on – and that's good enough.

When in your middle years, you were concerned with your appearance. But now who cares, there are other things to spend your time thinking about – for instance, am I warm enough? When you were born you were less complex and knew what you wanted. In your middle years, you got confused with the barrage of new toys, the image builders, and the paraphernalia of 'just have to have's'. In your old age, I got a telly, I got a dog, I got a bed, I get food, I got a daughter and son who love me, got lots of grandkids – got all I need. Less complex, more balance. The need to strive is gone.

As a child; when you had food in you, were dry and not tired, you were content – there was no scheming for more – nothing was missing – no greed or need for excess. When old: when you have food in you, are dry and not tired, you are content – no scheming for more – nothing is missing – no greed or need for excess.

Now, when you fall over, you get up, and yes, you may moan because it hurts, but you get on with it. Half the time you don't even bother to tell the family – this end of life can be tough but you don't cry over how hard it is? No you don't, as it is what it is and worrying about it can only make it worse.

As a newly-born, the thing that drove you was wonderment, now it is love. That is love of people, not love of things.

Old, you have more compassion, as you have been there, often. The middle years are too busy for compassion. The middle years are grabbing as much as possible. When old you share what you have.

A new born does not strive for identity – she is enough. The elderly know you are who you are because of what is inside of you, and that's all that matters.

Old people have no need to be small, they have unlearnt that.

You know that old people do not compare their achievements with others – what achievements they think about are another's, not their own. They talk about their family, not the possessions they had.

Middle aged people are searching for a God, or to prove there is not one. Old people just know and accept.

Being old, you learnt to see people, not what they were wearing. You saw their pain, not yours. You gave, and not caring about receiving. You think about them, not yourself.

You do not see yourself as being better than others. Nor do you think they are better than you – you know that no one is better than anyone else.

You learnt that irrespective of failures you still are good enough – no one can take that away from you – you know all is perfect just as you are.

13 October

We were asked to come in and see the facility manager today and learnt the following. Dad is still their most disruptive guest in the facility. When he is good, he is OK, but when bad he is intolerable; where he spits, punches and kicks staff. Most are adept but even so, on occasions they get spat in the eye, or kicked in the groin. Sadly they are running out of patience with him and it could be that they shunt him off to a facility in Hobart where they are better able to cope with this type of aggression. The manager continued to explain that even though the staff are trained they also get stressed with this type of continued behaviour.

They also asked us to supply more larger clothes as the normal fitting clothes are hard to put on him, whereas the jumbo size go on with less of a performance from Dad.

OH HELL

Bloody lucky, if you ask me.

He is snoring, one leg hanging off the bed, and angled down to the floor. He looks uncomfortable, but if we re-position him, he squirms back to the same position.

How can a man of his disposition have such good ladies in his life? This thought started because I found a photo album in his room. This contained about fifty black and white photos. They were of his early life, up to the end of the war. The photos of his family suggested a close and loving family. And then there were others of Dad on his own, where he is stage-posed, with a strut that suggested a supreme egotist. But there were also others, where he was with young ladies, about four different photos and four different woman. At the back would be something like Lech/Gretchen 1939. And it was these photos that prompted my wonderment. But I shall return to this thought in a moment.

What was strange about the photo album, which was very old, was that neither Helen or Mum (Enid) claimed to had ever laid eyes on it. It would seem through the twelve years of marriage to Mum, and the forty-five years with Helen that he had concealed it. For what purpose, did he do this? So secretive.

Now back to the woman of his life.

His first main relationship would have been with Hildegard. And by all accounts what a wonderful woman she was. Remember the respect that Joe had for Hilda, even though they had been divorced some twenty-seven years. Clearly she earned that respect, and so Dad would have experienced and benefited enormously from a life with Hilda.

And then there was Enid, loving, intelligent and caring, a real home maker.

And lastly Helen, who idolised and mollycoddled Dad.

He may have had the war years, but he had three amazing woman.

Yes, bloody lucky was he.

But so was I, and John. We also had Hilda as our biological mother, and Enid as the mother who raised us.

15th October

Three times in the last three days Helen has been to the shop for toilet paper, but always returned without and so we are now in the precarious situation of being down to the last few sheets. Today I joke with Helen by saying, "Perhaps I should place a sign on your chest, saying, please ask me if I have toilet paper, so that when she is going through the checkout the cashier can ask her "Do you have toilet paper?""

I was sitting on the beach watching him. It was one of those clear winter days in Sydney, where the westerly wind blows cold but clear so that headlands in the distance are sharp and the colours firm. It was a Saturday afternoon, a rare one where he was not drunk. I was about twelve and had wandered home from soccer as he was packing to go fishing.

Into his basket went the lead sinkers that he has smeltered that morning. The house still stunk metallic-like as he did this on the kitchen stove. Hooks of all sizes, methodically placed in clear glass jars, a knife recently sharpened, Vaseline to keep the moving parts of his stainless-steel reel running smoothly, spare fishing line, bags to insert the caught fish in, bait and cutting board, and of course cigarettes and his lighter, which he had had for many years. Picking up the basket in the one hand and the separated fishing rod that he had meticulously made himself in the other, he asked, "Vanna come fishen?"

When the westerlies blew, there was never any surf and so with nothing else to do I headed off with him. Those long legs of his swooped over the ground, and as we walked the narrow track, I was behind him and had to do a double-step every so often to keep up. Seems that walking and talking are not done at the same time, so it was in silence. But that was okay as I was always happy to be in the daydream of my head.

On this particular day it was beach fishing as opposed to the fishing from the rocks. I do not know what insight he had, but more often than not he was right and so caught fish.

Arriving on the beach, he turned right and headed to towards South Curl Curl, and went about a third of the way along. We passed a few people, a nod was offered.

Placing the basket on the sand, he assembled the two pieces of the rod together and attached the reel – its full length was about four metres long. Then standing the rod in the sand, he got the bait out and baited the hook. When ready, he walked the bazooka-like rod towards the edge of the water, leaned backwards and in one synchronised movement flicked the rod forward, where sinker and hook could be seen rocketing towards the horizon. Once the hook and sinker hit the water, he would give more line to let it sink towards the bottom. Then he would let more line out so he could walk backwards to the dryer sand. It was then that he would stand the rod in the sand, light a cigarette, and wait. Still no words were passed between us as he was absorbed in the experience of beach, sand, blue sky, seagulls and cigarette.

Every so often he would test the tension of the line by giving a slight tug, and perhaps every fifteen minutes or so he would reel the line in to check his bait. I knew that if there were fish about that he would catch some. From the beach he aimed for flathead – although bony, it's a sweet flavoured fish, and one of my favourites.

He was patient and hours would pass, with him only packing up when it was getting dark. On this occasion he caught about half a dozen flatties. He cleaned and filleted them on the water's edge so that the mess stayed on the beach and not in the kitchen at home. Already I could smell the fish cooking ...

Most often on those days, he would not get drunk, it's as if the exposure to nature was intoxicating enough. They were good days.

17th October

A different perspective on life happen today. I flew from Tasmania to Melbourne – from hospitals and death to life and expansion, from dementia to creative expression, from end of life issues to the exuberance of a young family. I went to visit Kim, Tim and my lovely granddaughter Esme-Rose. Today it is Kim's birthday. But not only that, in three days time, Tim and Kim are getting married. What a lovely prospect.

31 October

You can see by the date that I have not posted much of late, and that is because there has been just more of the same.

Helen seemed to be improving until I went to Melbourne for those five days. When I returned, she claimed that she was fine. But the reality was different. The anxiety was back to its worst, as is the memory.

A month ago she pulled everything out of the garden shed and gave it a good clean up. This was also with the idea of discarding old implements and accumulated bits and pieces that were no longer of use. But today, I went outside, and all the contents of the shed were, yet again, strewn outside on the grass. "What are you doing Helen?"

"I'm cleaning the shed. It's not been done for years and I'm glad to do it as there is so much junk to throw out. It's an absolute mess."

"Great" was all I could say.

And remember the concrete cleaning? Well, six weeks later the fetish continues. Ours is still nice and clean (God I have been here so long,

OH HELL

I now call it ours), but now so are both the houses on either side of ours, as well as some of the houses behind us. She can't leave it alone. In fact last night we had a chat about this. Not one that I had prompted. She started by asking me if she felt it would be OK if she could go and ask next door if she could clean their garage. Imagine that!

I replied, "It would be a nice thing to offer, but they may not be interested as they may think that you are snooping".

She accepted this, but went on to say that life was so empty for her that she must keep herself busy so her mind does not ponder what it should not ponder.

So for now life is reduced to fetishes so as to give form to life.

I then suggested, "Would now be a good time to start that charity support work? What about helping Meals on Wheels?" She now thinks this a great idea, and so whilst the idea was still in her memory I phoned them and made arrangements to collect their forms and the police clearance.

When I spoke to the lady there, I gently suggested that it would not be a good idea for Helen to do any driving or to have to find addresses – this would spook her. So it was agreed that if Helen works for them, she will be the person who carries the meals into the house. Helen is delighted with the prospects. I'll organise the forms this afternoon if I can pin her down.

And as for Dad. No real change. Days drift into meaningless days.

When I visited today, he was clutching his fluffy toy dog. Dolls and toy animals are given to the demented as they see them as real and bond to them. When they gave Dad the dog, it took two months for him to bond to it, but now he does, and holds it for hours a day. It is white and very fluffy and I thought it cute, that is, until he blew his nose on it.

Within his rambling, he said "It is fast".

"What's fast Dad?"

"Yes", he said

I think that he was referring to the toy dog.

Some fifteen minutes later he said, "He's coming home with me".

"Dad who is coming home with you?"

"Yes"

"Dad, where is home?"

"Hmmm"

"Is the dog coming home with you?"

Frère Jacques, Frère Jacques Dormez-vous? Dormez-vous ? Sonnez les matinées, sonnez les matinées Ding dang dong, ding dang dong...

I was so appreciative of one of the nurses, Mary. There was a tin of chocolates in his room and when I asked Mary who got them, she quietly said it was her. She said that she knows Dad likes chocolates and so bought them. She went on to say that she bought that specific brand as each chockie was individually wrapped – she thought Dad would derive a benefit, and busy him by unwrapping them. But, that did not work as he put the chocolates into his mouth, wrapping and all.

OH HELL

6 November

Difficult times ahead for Helen. Months ago I had offered to look after Kim and Tim's house and their dog Cooper whilst they were in South Africa visiting family. Because of the circumstances Kim tried to get someone else but they could not find anyone to take my place. Helen is brave, but I can see the underlying panic.

But somehow, sometime, she is going to have to look after herself, or go into a care facility. Now is a good time to test her ability and resolve to cope. Dad is controlled, and she does not see him anymore as it is too traumatic for her. I have cleared all doctors' and other appointments.

I called Alzheimer's Australia and asked them to drop in occasionally to keep an eye on her. I also asked Deborah to watch out. I will also phone Helen every couple of days. I know her so well by now that I can tell from her voice just where she is. If she gets too bad, then Cooper will just have to come back with me.

Thinking it may be good to try and busy her, whilst I am away, for the twentieth time I asked her if she wanted to get the Meals on Wheels papers out to fill out.

"No, I don't want the bother with a police clearance."

It is not that she has a record, it is just the thought of doing this seems too much for her. I did not push it, as she is too fragile to cause ructions.

8th November - Reflections

When I used to run long distance, there was a race that I ran nine times, called The Comrades Marathon. The race is well known in South Africa and is around ninety kilometres long, depending on road condition and changes. When almost every participant came in they were in such pain and so tired that when asked if they will run again next year, most would say "No". But the mind is a funny thing, and no matter how bad the pain was, its severity diminishes over time. And diminish it does, otherwise no one would run the race again.

Childbirth, I am told is also like this for the mother. If mothers were able to retain the absolute feeling of the pain they had when giving birth, I doubt that we as a species would have endured. But we did.

Old people; I am sure that if most knew what their last five or ten years of life would be like, to the absolute degree, then most would not want to get old and would try and avoid it.

I remember Dad mumbling (when in a period of lucidity) to himself months ago when he first went to hospital, "I yoi yoi", (he often said this when exasperated), "how did I let myself get here?" meaning old and mentally debilitated.

In these months, I have seen the old in pain, weary, demented, incontinent and covered in excrement, shouted at, abandoned, treated like imbeciles, (this I must add was never in the care facility where Dad is, but elsewhere), deaf or virtually deaf, weak of eyesight, where they are humbled beyond reason, bed bound, full of bed sores, in pain but unable to express it, bored and frustrated. How sad for them and for us to come. But worst for them is that when they are at that stage, it is never going to get better. Their only hope is where all is numbed through diminished capacity or drugs, and then relief with death.

Dad is suffering from bedsores. His skin is a watered down insipid milky colour. The sores won't go and get bigger all the time. Apparently they are quite painful.

Life was never meant to be fair. I remember the saying, by Dr Wayne Dyer, that if life was fair, then birds would not eat worms. Fifty and a hundred years ago, we let people die. Now we keep them alive, through months of suffering. Not sure that is smart. Of course there is a better way, but the politicians, especially in this country, do not have the fortitude to open that debate.

But life is precious and most will live it given the chance, and even with the loss of dignity that Dad may feel, I would still believe that at this stage he would not want a supported death. And nor would I at this stage – he is not in any real pain.

26th November

I'm in Melbourne for this short spell, and damn it, I got a call from the care facility, "Your dad's fading".

Shit

"But he should hang around another four or five days."

"Okay, thanks for letting me know, I will get back as soon as I can." So I booked to go back to Tasmania tomorrow afternoon. With Cooper I can't get on tonight's boat.

I then phoned Helen and told her that it looks like Dad is in his final week. She was good on the phone and said that she had seen him the day before and that she thought that he had turned that last corner. I gave her my arrival time and she was glad I was returning.

27th November

Another call from the facility, "Mr Grayson, I am sorry to tell you that..."

I should have been there. Bugger. I'm there for nearly seven months and I pop across to Melbourne and he goes. I'm not there, bugger, bugger.

I then thought about how to tell Helen. If I told her then, she would have been on her own and that would not be good. I had asked the care facility to not phone Helen, and I also called the funeral parlour with the same request, so I was confident she would not know. My arrival was at 8:00am the following morning. I would tell her then.

28th November

I arrived and woke Helen up. I let her get the sleepy dust out of her eyes. When I felt she was ready, I took her one hand and simply said, "Dad, is gone. He went yesterday." I waited for her to take it in, which she did with strength and dignity. The fact that Dad had been out of the house for the last seven months helped, and that she has already been grieving for all that time.

I gave her a tissue, and then continued, "He died at around 2:30 yesterday afternoon. I could have phoned you and told you then but I didn't want you to have the news and spend the night on your own. I hope that I did the right thing?"

"Thank you, I am glad you waited until you came, it is best this way."

I then made her a cup of tea and we just sat, mainly in silence. There was the occasional sniffle from her. But once the tea was gone, she got up and said, "I must organise my breakfast". This I felt was to satisfy a need to be busy, and not to assuage hunger.

OH HELL

The rest of her day was keeping herself busy, and so more concrete was washed, this time up the road. But another function was embarked upon. She got out her ladder. Now this is not any ladder, it is 'the ladder' that her father had made for her some sixty years ago. To me it looked like a bunch of 4x2's nailed together to form a tripod, with more 4x2's nailed for steps. But no, "This was not like those cheap and nasty aluminum ladders that you buy from the stores. This is a ladder that my father made. But you know, I would not lend it to anyone, as you have to know how to place your feet. Only I can use this ladder."

An hour later, she came in to tell me that she was going next door to clean their gutters. Oh no, here we go again...

29th November

Off to the funeral parlour for two hours. Won't bore you with the details. But all the processes are finalised. Relatives contacted, condolences received... "and how are you feeling?" many asked.

"Oh I'm all right."

But later, I ask myself the same question, and acknowledge that I feel kind of weird, like I am not present. I'm functional, and not very emotional. I was not expecting to be, after all Dad was Dad and what is there to get emotional about? Yet, something's stirred up, perhaps it is because Dad is my Dad. I've just decided it is wine-o-clock!

1st December

Sadly, over the last few days Helen has regressed and her memory terrible. We had a meeting with the celebrant, and at least six times before the celebrant arrived, Helen asked, "What is this appointment about?" Then when the celebrant arrived and I called Helen, she came in and was baffled as to who was there and why.

2nd December

Not a good day. Helen went out to the nursery to get some plants and do some shopping. This was mainly to keep herself busy. I expected her to be out about two hours, but after three she was still not back. But soon thereafter a car pulled up at the curb and a tearful Helen emerged. I wondered where her car was. I soon find out, "I lost the car".

Helen, after finishing at the last shop tried to return to the car, but she could not find it. She walked around and around looking for it, having absolutely no memory of where it could be. Poor old thing. Anyway, two ladies saw her crying and asked her if they could help. Helen told them and asked if they would bring her home to me, which they did. Luckily, I was using Deborah's car as she is away on the main land, and so off we went to find the delinquent vehicle. It took an hour, but in the end there it was in a parking lot.

When we get home, she simmers down and starts to process the post that had come today. Coming to me she asks, "What do you think this means?"

Taking the letter I saw; YOUR PENSION WAS SUSPENDED AS OF THE 23RD NOVEMBER 2015.

Well that is clear enough I thought. Reading the rest, it seemed that Centrelink, the government department that handles pensions had sent Helen a form to fill out. As she is incapable of doing this, it did not get done. So Centrelink sent another form but this one also said that it needs to be in by a certain date or her pension would be suspended. This letter was also ignored, so they suspended it. So off to the local branch of Centrelink to sort it out.

What is annoying or unfair, is that Centrelink do not seem take the mentally infirm into consideration. Luckily Helen has money in reserve, but there are many who don't. In fact, Helen would not have even known her pension had been suspended, and if she was like many others who live from fortnight to fortnight, she would have gone hungry.

I wonder how on earth will Helen cope when I leave. Yes, she is worse at the moment, and hopefully will settle, but still it is a concern.

5th December

Today Helen had lost her car keys. She had been out and about but when she returned she had no recollection where the keys were. By this time my daughter Kim and my brother John were here in preparation for the funeral, and so we all conducted a search, which did not reveal where they were. But later, it occurred to me to check in the pockets of some of the coats that Helen wears when she walks the dog in blustery and cold weather. I found the keys in a coat that I had never seen her wear, and so took the coat into the room where Helen was, still frantic and crying with agitation. I asked her, "When was the last time you wore this coat?"

"Not for months." I then pull the keys out of the pocket and showed her. She shook her head in amazement because she had no memory of wearing that coat for a long time.

After this, still upset, she decided to reclaim some control over her environment. She opened the refrigerator, which was chock-a-block with food in preparation for the people who are coming for the funeral. What she did was to get clear plastic bags and labels to label the food. For obscure items in Tupperware containers this was probably a good idea but it was sad to see the carrots as being marked carrots even though they could be seen through the clear plastic. The same with cauliflower and all the other vegetables. When I told Kim this, she had tears in her eyes.

8th December

Today was the day of the funeral. I shall not elaborate on this as I'm sure you're not likely to have much interest in it, suffice to say that it went off very well and Helen got through the day with strength and poise. She was pleased with the arrangements and all that had been done. But before the funeral when she emerged from her bedroom in the same clothes that she had been going into town for shopping or other chores, which it is to say they were quite grubby. She looked decidedly unkempt. I did not say anything as I felt she had enough to deal with. Nor did anybody else comment on it so I was grateful for their respect.

11th December

These last two days since the funeral Helen has been wonderful. She has been intelligent, and short term memory functioning relatively well. Perhaps I have been wrong with my assessment as to how she will get on. As she was doing so well I chatted to her to determine when I should leave. I made the suggestion that I stay for a further three weeks in the hope that she will be as settled as she can be. This period would also encompass three important dates, these being; Dad's birthday, Christmas Day and her birthday. I told her that for these I did not want her to be on her own. She agreed, and so my time here is nearly over.

OH HELL

16 December

Not much to report, Helen is more stable, but has periods of extreme forgetfulness.

The ashes are ready, and I put the three choices to Helen. The first is, once collected; do we scatter them somewhere, such as over the ocean near where Dad used to fish? The second option is where the funeral directors buries them under the plaque? The third is similar to the last but we do the burying? Helen liked this last option best, mainly because for many years of Dad's life he did not have a place he really called home, and that he was itinerant for large chunks of his life and so the placing of his ashes in one place would have pleased him.

18th December

I had been wanting to buy a car, and as there was no hurry, I was looking at the best possible buy and price. I had ascertained the type of vehicle to best suit my bohemian lifestyle, and lo and behold, there was one perfect option at an estate auction. I did my research on the car, determined what the value should be for that model and year. And so Helen and I went to the auction.

When the car came up, I ensconced myself right under the auctioneers stand, so I could clearly hear him, but more importantly so he could see me and my bids. I had found out that there was no reserve on the car and so the auctioneer started by announcing, do we have a bid of X amount, This was roughly the amount that I deemed the car value to be.

I then made a bid of half of that, and waited, I then heard him say we have a bid from the lady at the back, which was a few hundred dollars more than mine. Then a third bid came in from another bidder so I shouted out another bid, the lady raised her bid again.

I was focusing on the words of the auctioneers and the bid amounts and so was not watching the other bidder, when I heard the auctioneer say, "Hang on, aren't you the mother of this bidder?" I then looked through the crowd, and saw that it was Helen who was the lady in the back. Fortunately the auctioneer had seen us as we came in and assumed that the she was my mother, so he said, "Simple mistake, we will return to this man's first bid." So then I bid against a few other people and finally won the bid at roughly 55% of the perceived value, so I was delighted.

Later when I saw Helen, I asked her why she bid against me, she said, "Well I was helping you get the car as I know you want it".

She also had bid, and won on three other occasions, so she came home with an assortment of ceramic ornaments, a candle set of a Chinese man and woman. These will have to find a home in this house which already looks like a museum.

21st December

I have noticed of late that Helen is having more and more difficulty spelling. Throughout her life her spelling has been impeccable, well it had to be as a teacher. Now she struggles much like a dyslexic. I should know as I am one, and always have had great difficulty. Being dyslexic forced me to leave school at the earliest legal age. There are times in a document where I may spell a recurring word five different ways but each spelling looks correct. When I try and spell some words it is like the connections in the brain are not there and no matter how hard I try, the spelling will not come. Now I see the same with Helen, the spelling will not come. Sadly, this seems to be getting worse.

Knowing how much administration there was to get through, I planned to leave Helen and Tasmania halfway through January.

OH HELL

When at the Accountant and the lawyer yesterday, both gave a list of needs, and with each one Helen got more and more confused. So I said, "Don't worry, I will do these before I go". But with many offices closed and the slowdown for Christmas I felt that I needed those extra few weeks to get through it all. When I had told Helen this yesterday, she agreed the timing would be good, and reiterated that there is no way she can do the admin. But today the winds blew from a different direction.

She came to me and asked if we could talk. This usually entailed going into the lounge room with a cup of tea. Once seated, she bluntly said, "When do you think that you will have caught up with the admin (said as if I was a paid employee), as I need to be on my own?"

"Well, as I said the yesterday it's likely to take a few more weeks. Why do you ask?"

"I want you to go, and as soon as possible. I know it's Christmas but could you try and get on the first boat?"

That's blunt I thought.

She continued, "I think I am well enough. When can you look at booking?"

Taken aback, I said "I'm working on something at the moment, I'll have a look this afternoon".

"Please can you look now?"

"Helen, would it not be better if I got the admin up to date first? After all, you know you can't cope with it, nor do you want to cope with it. Part of the reason why it will take me longer is because of the Christmas slowdown, and also that when I need you to help me, you can only focus for a short period of time. I don't want to put pressure on you, so we have to pace it accordingly?"

"I know, but I have to do it all myself and want to start. I can do it all myself and I don't need you anymore."

Indignantly I rose to leave the room, I said, "OK, I'll go on-line and do it now".

In my bedroom, come office, I sat on the bed and was pissed off. Fuck, I thought. I have just given eight and a half months of my life away to support her and this is how she wants to end it, seemingly without gratitude for all that I had done? Obviously I was there to help. It was not about payment or pats on the back, but this attitude annoyed me. Well bugger her, I will book and go ASAP.

But later, once I had simmered down, I could understand that this, almost belligerent, and irrational behaviour, is a typical symptom of advancing dementia. But even so, she is still in charge of her life, I had to respect that and acquiescent to her request.

But there was another reason why I knew I needed to leave now, and that is that Helen must be on her own to fumble in her attempt to clutch at independence, or to crash and burn, in which case I would return and get her into an institution. For the later to happen, she would have to ask for that.

27th December

The car was packed and it was time to leave. Helen walked out with me to say goodbye. After a quick hug, she placed her skeletal hand on my shoulder. With a squeeze she said, "Thank you. I could not have survived this without you".

As I drove around the corner, I had one final glance and wave, Zoe at her feet – Helen's forty kilograms buffeted by the wind. Raising her arm, seemingly without enthusiasm, scared but determined. I am sure that at that moment we both had the same thought, how on earth will she withstand the difficulties that she is likely to endure.

OH HELL
Final say

This diary and story could go on but I will end it here.

Lou and Hildegard were victims of their era. Their lives and that era are now closed. Both their lives were dictated by six years of war. Six years that instilled Post Traumatic Stress Syndrome that ruled their lives. But in that crazy time, they clung to each other, trying desperately to make certain what had been uncertain. But they split and exploded into a million fragments, I am one of those fragments, as are my siblings. As one of those fragment, I seen the effect that it had and marvel at the curious thing, where a hand full of war years determines the rest of a life.

It was not all bad though, and both had many reasons for happiness; Helen gave peace and contentment to Dad for forty-five years; and Hilda had her children and grandchildren. For both of them there would have been much to have been happy with.

Dad – now that your Demons are stilled, the confusion gone – it is my wish that you are now on the veranda of your beloved farm, a glass of red wine by your side, Zoe at your feet, as you overlook the damn, enjoying the birds as they flit around in the yellowing light of sunset. And Helen is close by, forever fussing around you...

Hilda – you left a long brood behind you. You are loved by many.

Enid – a blessing, sent to save John and I.

Me – how can I measure and quantify all the thoughts that have bombarded me since I received that first SMS from Kim? I can't, well not yet anyway. This experience in some ways heightened the confusion. This book has helped. As you saw, I had a difficult early life, but I have much to be grateful for as there were far more blessings than detriments.

After rereading the manuscript, one thing jumped out at me; that perhaps I could have tried harder for Dad, and especially Helen. But then I realised that the disease of dementia brings out the best and worst in the family members who take on the role to look after demented family members. Throughout the writing of this, I did not try and hide my frustration or present it to you in a better light. Yes, there were times when I was frustrated, and so will you be if you find yourself in a similar situation. The wise words of James A. Michener in his book *Recessional* are apt here; "When you work with Alzheimer's families you learn what love is, what terror can be, and what nothingness in life in certain forms can mean". As the career you would be a rare species to not be affected by that.

The funeral

A gram of family is worth a ton of gold.

They came, partly to honour Dad, but more so because they are family, and family supports family. That is, good families do, and ours is a good family.

Bonding through compassion, there to offer the best they can carry, which is themselves, when the chips are down they are here in an instant, offering support, money, shoulders to cry on and arms for hugging.

Family members are not necessarily blood relatives, they are family through their care, conforming to no laws, a belonging and making others feel they belong, supported and supporting.

Family is a true blessing – our family is a true blessing.

Permission from Helen

When I started to write this book, I spoke to Helen and asked her if I could relate what she has been through. Upon hearing what I said she was insistent and in that forthright way said, "I'm sure that I am not the only one to be going through this and so it may help others". Then recently, when editing the manuscript I reiterated that I had written it and she confirmed that her difficulties must not be glossed over in any way, that it must be reflected candidly.

Dad's eulogy

When it was time to write this I had no intention of including negativity in this. After all, no one should go off with the last words being of negativity. Yet, afterwards, two of the brothers mentioned to me, "good eulogy, nice fabrication".

This is what I said:

How does one know the moon? Daily it's presented before us, but yet we still do not know it.

And the breeze, what does its whispering mean? It talks, but of what?

There are many mysteries to life. Alas, our father was one. In fact, for us kids; Keith, John, Steve and myself; he couldn't have been more alien if he tried – we knew so little about him. And now he is gone just short of his ninety-third birthday, and we still are none the wiser as to who he was. Perhaps it was meant to be that way?

But the little that we do know I shall relate. He was born in 1922 in Poland, but in a region that had strong German influence and sentiment. We know virtually nothing of his years there, other than the fact that he was much influenced by the German culture.

However, as a youngster his family moved to Imphy in France, as there was no work in Poland in those years of Depression.

His father (our grandfather) was a part-time musician, playing at night and through the day we believe he was a fitter and turner, which is what Dad became.

From what I can gather, his time in France was not a happy time, because with the surname Grundkowski he was bullied. However, in the few instances he spoke about it, it was with fondness. Imphy, a pretty little town on the banks of a meandering river seemed to be a good place for Dad to grow up, where he played soccer, and also competed in cycle races. It would seem that he was very good at these. We know because he told us! When a kid, you tend to believe what your parents tell you.

And it was here in this little town that Dad was indentured, to learn the trade of fitting and turning. His father also wanted Dad to be a musician but Dad had no interest, he loved using his hands and his initiative in his new trade. This love for what he did seemed to make him a better than average tradesman, whereby he played his metal lath with the dexterity and gentleness that Grandfather play the violin.

The war came and interrupted life, and Dad, along with his dad went to Germany and enlisted. I know nothing about our Grandfather's events in the war, but Dad landed up in a mechanical division. This was safer than being on the front lines, being cannon fodder for that insane Hitler. Indeed, details are virtually non-existent. But what we did learn, which would usually come out in moments of inebriation, was that he found himself in that most horrific of campaigns in Stalingrad.

For many war historians, this was one of the worst and bloodiest throughout the Second World War. 300,000 German troops went there to try and conquer Russia, but only a handful returned. I won't make this a history lesson, suffice to say, that it is well-known that most of those who survived, walked from Stalingrad back to Germany, a distance of some 2000 km. The hardships and the starvation in that horrific time, not to mention the severity of the winter, would have been more than most could bear – only the most strong willed survived. It is this strength of will, which categorised a stubbornness in Dad that sometimes belied logic.

I must pause here to be thankful that his stubbiness skipped a generation...

Once again, details are sketchy, but it would seem that by the time he got back to Germany, the US forces had arrived and so Dad found himself in a prisoner of war camp. But after a time, I think Dad pragmatically reclaimed his Polish nationality and told the authorities that he was forced into the German army. This was believable as many were press ganged into the services.

Once out of the POW camp, and with the war over, he was a free citizen living in Germany. And for some of this time, he was in Munich, which at the start of the war, was the main centre for Nazism in Germany, and it was the home of that infamous death camp 'Dachau'. But it was also the home of Hildegard, the lady who became my and John's mother and Dad's wife, his first of three wives. They, both of them, with minds ravaged from the hideous events of the war wanted to escape the grimness of broken Europe and so headed for Australia. Upon landing on these shores, neither set foot out of the country again, nor did either want to ever return to Europe. However, I think that they both learnt that you can escape a land, but your demons travel with you.

Both were good immigrants and loved this country and what it offered. But with those shattered emotions, it was unlikely that my mother and father would stay together and so they drifted apart. Dad had good and secure employment and it would seem that his skills as a tradesman were well appreciate it. But it was still a dark time for him, where he tried to douse those war-time images with copious quantities of alcohol. A pattern emerged, where from Friday evening, until Sunday evening, he was anaesthetised. But come Monday morning, he would be back at work, reliable and dedicated.

This was the Dad that we four kids grew up with. He was distant and introverted, except for those weekends, where often times he was belligerent and difficult. Yet, he never spent time away from the home and family, and always provided as well as possible.

But there was one glimmer of sunlight in his life, and that was fishing. He loved to fish, whether it was off the rocks at headlands, or casting out miles from a sandy beach, or the tranquillity of being in a row boat and rowing out into some quiet bay. When fishing, we saw more of who he really was, he was more present to us, and his surrounds. But not only that, we grew up loving fish as there was always an abundance of them. There was one such time when Dad took John, Keith and I camping for the weekend. Seems like there was not much food taken but of course there was beer! It did not take long for Dad to net a feast of prawns, and so we imbibed on these succulent creatures and a glass of beer each.

He would make his own fishing rods from scratch, great long things, that to us kids seemed as tall as a telegraph pole. And his sinkers, he had his own smelting works in the kitchen, using the gas stove, and often times we would be shooed out as his sinker production was in full swing. The kitchen for the rest of the day would pong of molten lead. It's a wonder he did not die at thirty-five of lead poisoning.

Growing up we would ask him about his early days – he always changed the subject. He refused to talk about his family, which was odd as they seemed to be functional and loving. He certainly would not talk about the war.

And then later, some thirty years ago, I made mention to Helen of my 'itching' to know more of his past, and of course his time in the war. Although she sympathised with me, she asked me not to dig, because digging upsets him. Recognising her wisdom and compassion I had to suppress my intrigue – damn!! So I promised her that I wouldn't, nor did I.

In about 1970 Dad got a job at the Savage River Mine and so it was to this state of Tasmania that he came, and fell in love with. It was also here that he met a young school teacher, Helen Diers.

OH HELL

Dad was a bit of a loner, preferring his own company. But what is the happiest thing for one loner to do... it's to meet another loner and so Helen traded her maiden name Diers for Grayson. This was around forty years ago. The number of years is dependent on when the question is asked, as tomorrow's answer is likely to be different from yesterday's. But in Helen's words, who cares about the years when you are enjoying life! Anyway, an odd but enduring relationship was formed, especially when it was discovered that loner number two, fell in love with fishing, which was a happy backdrop for many weekends away for them.

Early on, they had agreed, that from a social contact point of view that they were pretty much self-sufficient. It was not that they discouraged friendships, as there were some, but they could go literally weeks without a visitor and they were good with that, that is, as long as they had each other. And when they bought the land at Squeaking Point they divvied up the work-load according to their likes and skills, where each tinkered around with what they wanted to do. Helen was the farmer, and Dad the instrument and machinery expert. Dad drove the tractor, but Helen picked up the potatoes. Helen was the house manager, cook and washer-upper, Dad,... well Dad sat and drank wine or read his book, or both. However, he did help with the washing up at night and cooked Helen's breakfast on Saturday mornings.

But in this relationship, if perchance, one would encroach upon the domain of the other ... well! Skirmishes happened, with Dad uttering, Gott or Mightly (translated as God all Mighty) and Helen, with pursed lips, would storm back to her domain and both would get on with it. An hour or so later, at lunch or a break, all was forgotten and harmony restored.

But I cannot continue without speaking of some of the other faux pas that Dad had with his use of English. After Hildegard departed, and between Helen, there was Enid. Enid is now ninety-two, which is amazing considering the four active boys she raised. Enid and Dad were together for about fourteen years.

Enid, or rather Mum, is the mother John and I needed, she was the mum Dad wanted for us. Mum tells the story, where, at a relatively sophisticated dinner party, Dad, after a few drinks found his voice; and somehow the conversation got round to dental issues. Dad was always very proud of his 'teats', as he called them, but when he started talking about Enid's teats, and that they hang all over the place, apparently there was either raucous laughter or incredulous expressions. Dad never quite understood why everybody was laughing or of Mum's embarrassment.

And then there is Deborah. Deborah was nursing at Burnie hospital and has become a good friend. Deborah was often summonsed by Dad, shouting, so half the hospital could hear, "Zebboror, Zebboror, kom, I need to pee".

Anyway, to continue, the fact is that Dad, and Helen are both very simple people, with simple needs, with no need for the grandiose.

I've mentioned several times of Dad's skill as a machinist. But his crowning glory would have been when he was working at Savage River, a repair was required to a trunnion bearing. This stainless steel, house sized bearing, developed cracks. Management were to dismantle it and ship it to the main land for repairs, a massive undertaking, given its size, not to mention the costs. Dad went to management suggesting that he could repair it. His plan was to have a scaffold raised against the bearing and place his lath as well as a seven ton drill loaded on it. From there he would do the work. So for several weeks he worked long shifts on the scaffold, and soon enough the bearing was good as new. For this, he was given a written commendation for his ingenuity, as well as a photo in the paper. For him 99.9% was not good enough, it had to be 100% or nothing. I also suspect that when totally focused on his work, as he always was, it was the only time that the war years did not intrude his thoughts.

 The Dad in his the latter years was a much gentler, and a more kind hearted dad than of our growing up years. For this gentleness to have emerged, it must have always been there – hidden under the weight of war memories. The fact was that the war years never really left him, always an overriding shadow. But fortunately, there were two things that helped to coach out this more gentle aspect. One was; that with each passing year he was distanced from the war, and so the tension and strain would slightly diminish. But I suspect that the main reason was Helen and her supporting gentle nature. It was she who coached that shy animal out from its hiding place. Thank you Helen, for all that you have done for our father.

In these months leading up to Dad's final passing, I saw a man who was vastly different from the one who we grew up with. Yes, he was irascible as the elderly can be and still demanding, "Zebboror, I need a pee". But there was an undertone of affection and gentler way about him.

But still, he was a mystery.

And so Dad, from myself, and the rest of the family, may you rest in peace and that your demons have also been laid to rest.

www.ingramcontent.com/pod-product-compliance
Lightning Source LLC
Chambersburg PA
CBHW050451010526
44118CB00013B/1787